THE SMALL GARDEN

THE SMALL GARDEN

SUE AND ROGER NORMAN · POLLY BOLTON · LALLIE COX

Illustrations by
ELAINE FRANKS

This edition published by Parragon, 1999
Parragon
Queen Street House
4 Queen Street
Bath BA1 1HE

Produced by
Robert Ditchfield Ltd
Combe Court, Kerry's Gate
Hereford HR2 0AH

ISBN 0 75252 558 1

A copy of the British Library Cataloguing in Publication Data is available from the Library.

Typeset by Action Publishing Technology Ltd, Gloucester
Colour origination by Mandarin Offset Ltd, Hong Kong
Printed and bound in Italy

ACKNOWLEDGEMENTS

Many of the photographs have been taken in the gardens and nurseries of the authors at Marley Bank, Whitbourne,
Bromyard (Sue and Roger Norman), Nordybank Nurseries, Clee St Margaret (Polly Bolton), Woodpeckers, Marlcliff,
Bidford-on-Avon (Lallie Cox). The publishers would also like to thank the many people and organizations who have
allowed photographs to be taken for this book, including the following:

Acton Beauchamp Roses, Worcester; Mr and Mrs Terence Aggett; Mrs Anthony Anderson; Barnsley House; Batemans
(National Trust); Bromesberrow Place; Burford House, Tenbury Wells; Dinmore Manor; Richard Edwards, Well Cottage,
Blakemere; Haseley Court; Mrs G.A. Follis; Lance Hattatt, Arrow Cottage, Weobley; The Hon Mrs Peter Healing, The
Priory, Kemerton; Mr and Mrs James Hepworth, Elton Hall; Hergest Croft Gardens; Hill Court, Ross-on-Wye; Mr and
Mrs B. Howe; Mrs R. Humphries, Orchard Bungalow, Bishops Frome; Kim Hurst, The Cottage Herbery, Boraston Ford;
Mrs David Lewis, Ash Farm, Much Birch; Mrs M.T. Lloyd, Edenbridge House; Misarden Park; Mottisfont Rose Gardens
(National Trust); Mrs E.A. Nelson; Mrs R. Paice, Bourton House; Mrs G.M. Pennington; Pentwyn Cottage Garden, Bacton;
The Picton Garden, Colwall; Powis Castle (National Trust); Mrs Clive Richards, Lower Hope, Ullingswick; RHS Garden,
Wisley; Rose Cottage, Aldbourne; Royal Botanic Gardens, Kew; Malcolm Skinner, Eastgrove Cottage Gardens, Shrawley;
Snowshill (National Trust); Stone House Cottage, Kidderminster; Malley Terry, 28 Hillgrove Crescent, Kidderminster;
Raymond Treasure, Stockton Bury Farm, Kimbolton; Mrs Trevor-Jones, Preen Manor; The Trumpet Inn, Evesham;
Wakehurst Place (National Trust); David Wheeler, The Neuadd; Mrs Geoffrey Williams, Close Farm, Crockham Hill; Mr
and Mrs R. Williams; Mrs David Williams-Thomas, The Manor House, Birlingham; Woodlands, Bridstow; Wyevale
Garden Centre, Hereford; York Gate, Leeds.

We would like to thank especially Mrs D.L. Bott and Queenswood Garden Centre, Wellington, Hereford for their help.

Photographs of sweet pea 'Bijou Mixed' and *Impatiens* 'Picotee Swirl' are reproduced by kind permission of Thompson &
Morgan Ltd., Ipswich, Suffolk.

CONTENTS

How to Use This Book

Where appropriate, approximate measurements of a plant's height have been given, and also the spread where this is significant, in both metric and imperial measures. The height is the first measurement, as for example 1.2m × 60cm/4 × 2ft. However, both height and spread vary so greatly from garden to garden since they depend on soil, climate and position, that these measurements are offered as guides only. This is especially true of trees and shrubs where ultimate growth can be unpredictable.

The following symbols are also used throughout the book:

    ○ = thrives best or only in full sun
    ◑ = thrives best or only in part-shade
    ● = succeeds in full shade
    E = evergreen

Where no sun symbol and no reference to sun or shade is made in the text, it can be assumed that the plant tolerates sun or light shade.

Plant Names

For ease of reference this book gives the botanical name under which a plant is most widely listed for the gardener. These names are sometimes changed and in such cases the new name has been included. Common names are given wherever they are in frequent use.

Poisonous Plants

In recent years, concern has been voiced about poisonous plants or plants which can cause allergic reactions if touched. The fact is that many plants are poisonous, some in a particular part, others in all their parts. For the sake of safety, it is always, without exception, essential to assume that no part of a plant should be eaten unless it is known, without any doubt whatsoever, that the plant or its part is edible and that it cannot provoke an allergic reaction in the individual person who samples it. It must also be remembered that some plants can cause severe dermatitis, blistering or an allergic reaction if touched, in some individuals and not in others. It is the responsibility of the individual to take all the above into account.

Water in the Garden

All water gardens are beautiful, but sadly they can be dangerous, mostly to children who can drown in even a few inches of water, or sometimes to adults. We would urge readers where necessary to take account of this and provide a reliable means of protection if they include water in the garden.

PATIOS, POTS AND WINDOW BOXES

A PATIO OR PAVED AREA next to your house can be a joy for ever, if you get it right. The site will usually dictate the materials to be used and plants that will grow best.

Away from the house, paved or terraced areas give much more freedom in the choice of plants and construction materials.

Think carefully how you want to use the area. If you want a barbecue, then more of your patio will need to provide a level, uncluttered space for tables and chairs. If it is to be used by children, then safe surfaces and few vulnerable pots will be required. If plants are to be the main interest, then the aspect of the site will dictate what will grow best.

You must consider your planting plans at the design stage. The range of choices is enormous. Crevice planting? Borders? Raised beds? Pots and containers? Water feature? Climbers?

Be careful to choose materials which blend or contrast effectively with the surroundings and which are practical. Do not use gravel where children run, or where it will be walked into the house, and beware of smooth surfaces in shaded areas; they can be very slippery in winter.

Be sure to use adequate foundations and that the area drains properly.

PLANTING PATIOS AND TERRACES

How you plant your paved area will depend a lot on how much time you have available to look after it. It is no use developing a mass planting scheme in pots and containers for summer colour on a hot patio if you are not going to be there to water it twice a day in high summer, although there are automatic watering systems which would help.

Planting in containers has the enormous advantage of flexibility. You can have different schemes throughout the year and can grow plants that would not grow in your garden soil.

Beds offer easier growing conditions – larger root runs and less demanding watering – but are less flexible. Raised beds offer the added dimension of height and can be filled with the soil of your choice.

Many plants like to grow in the gaps between paving. This environment gives a cool root run which does not dry out quickly and, if the gaps are filled with gravel, this ensures a dry area round the neck of the plant, which is much appreciated by many alpines. Areas which are heavily walked on require tougher, shorter plants.

This well-planted patio has room for a table and chairs beneath a pergola which provides shade and overhead colour from plants. It is sturdy enough to support hanging baskets.

(*Left*) A flight of steps shows off potted plants to advantage as it grades their heights. Here alyssum, violas, pansies, fuchsia and lobelia benefit from the shelter of the wall.

(*Opposite left*) A large tender *Aeonium arboreum* in a pot is put outside in summer. It leads the eye to Ali Baba jars planted with herbs on the steps.

CHOOSING POTS AND CONTAINERS

When choosing pots and containers it is important to consider how they will look in their surroundings and what plants you will put in them. Tall plants, especially in windy places, need broad-based containers. Alpines look best in sinks, troughs or shallow pans. Trailing plants need taller containers, such as chimney pots.

The range of pots and containers available to gardeners is enormous, from antique stone or lead cisterns to plastic pots. For those with a creative streak, almost anything can be adapted, provided it has drainage holes. If they are to be used outside in cold winter areas, containers must be frost resistant. Also, porous containers left outside in frosty conditions should be raised clear of solid surfaces on pieces of slate, or special ornamental feet.

PLANTING

Almost any plant can be grown in a container: even forest trees can be grown as Bonsai subjects. It is important to strike the right balance between size of plant, size of pot, compost strength and plant vigour. It is better to

repot a plant frequently than to put a small plant straight into a large container.

Loam-based composts are the easiest to use for plants in pots and containers; they hold moisture and fertilizers better than other composts. Possible exceptions to this are composts for hanging baskets and window boxes, where weight is an important consideration.

It is necessary to use an ericaceous compost for rhododendrons, azaleas, heathers and other lime-hating plants.

Most plants need feeding and this can be achieved by adding fertilizers to the compost

A row of trimmed box in pots gives the effect of a neat hedge.

(Above) An old lead cistern with pelargoniums and a purple cotinus.

(Left) A tiny terrace with scented lilies beside the seat.

and by liquid feeding when watering. Annuals and soft perennials planted closely to flower over a long period need a strong compost and frequent liquid feeds. Trees and shrubs need a compost with relatively large amounts of slow release fertilizer, liquid feeding and annual repotting. They can be maintained in their final containers for some years by removing annually in spring as much compost as possible, without too much root disturbance, and replacing with fresh compost containing controlled-release fertilizer. Trees and shrubs will also need pruning to give them shape and to improve flowering.

Plants in containers tend to dry out very quickly and need frequent watering. During hot summer periods, hanging baskets and some pots will need watering twice a day. Equipment can be used to help with watering. Additives are also available which are designed to retain water in the compost and to aid rewetting dried-out composts.

(Above) Red flowers are set off by foliage in this swagged pot under a hood.

(Right) A lovely and slightly tender *Abutilon megapotamicum*.

Most annuals and soft perennials need dead-heading regularly to keep them flowering throughout the season.

SITING

Pots and containers can be used in a variety of ways from the dramatic to the utilitarian. A group of herb-filled pots are an asset by the kitchen door or in a window box. Succulents and pelargoniums give a sunny corner a Mediterranean look, and a group of scented plants, either similar or contrasting, can be placed by a seat or along a narrow path. Pots can be used to disguise, or distract the eye from, unattractive features. Pots of lilies can be plunged in borders to fill gaps and enhance colour schemes. A large container can be used to dramatic effect as a focal point or as the centre piece in a formal border. An interesting container can be very effective even when unplanted. Containers can give emphasis to doors, gates, arches and steps.

13

1. PLANTING A PATIO

*A paved area can create a very special
climate for a range of plants you cannot
grow elsewhere.*

PAVING PLANTS

At the design stage specify lots of gaps for plants, but leave some room for people!

Small, self-seeding plants, like *Erinus alpinus* (Fairy foxglove) and *Inopsidium acaule* (Violet cress) thrive in paving cracks.

The green leaves, pinkish stems and white flowers of this stonecrop make a good combination. The full name of this plant is **Sedum album** ssp. **teretifolium** var. **murale** ○, 7.5 × 45cm/3in × 1½ft.

PLANTS IN THE GAPS BETWEEN PAVING soften the edges and add interest to your patio. Take care to leave clear walking areas. Thymes, creeping mints and chamomile may be planted on the edges of routes, as they tolerate bruising and are aromatic, whereas sempervivums are easily broken and do better in a sunny corner, out of the way of people's feet.

There are many varieties of **sempervivum (houseleeks)**, all of them decorative, even heraldic in shape with their evergreen rosettes and starry flowers in summer. After flowering, the individual rosette dies, but surrounding offsets continue. ○, E, 10cm/4in by indefinite spread.

DIANTHUS – PINKS – are amongst the prettiest small midsummer flowers and will grow well with their heads in the sun and their roots in the cool, moist conditions under the paving. Unless you are strictly a summer gardener you will want some interest at other seasons, such as spring bulbs, dwarf conifers and saxifrages which flower in spring and have attractive all-year foliage.

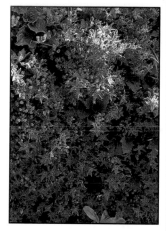

Campanula garganica
Beautiful, dwarf perennial with starry flowers ideally suited to a paving crevice, summer to autumn.
15 × 45cm/6in × 1½ft

Use a gravel that blends with your paving to cover the soil.

Endeavour to keep the gravel just below the paving level to minimize its spread by feet.

Old-fashioned pinks are very fragrant but have only one main flush of flowers. Modern varieties will flower recurrently if dead-headed regularly.

PAVING PLANTS

WHEN BUYING PLANTS to put between your paving you need to consider the size of the gap available. Small, young plants tend to establish more easily than larger, older ones. Whatever their size, ensure that they have sufficient soil for their roots to develop.

Campanula hallii Little white bells over good green foliage. 5 × 60cm/2in × 2ft

Androsace lanuginosa Clusters of blush or lilac-pink flowers mass the trailing mat of silky leaves. ○, 5 × 30cm/2in × 1ft

Scilla sibirica Easy spring bulb, blooming year after year, needing little attention. ◑, 10–15cm/4–6in tall

Campanula cochleariifolia var. *pallida* '**Miranda**' One of the very best with many slate-blue flowers. 5 × 60cm/2in × 2ft

Troughs combine well with paved areas, adding height and more planting opportunities. Pots, or ornaments, can be used to emphasize pathways and to lead the eye to the rest of the garden.

◆ *Almost fill the crevice with gravel round the neck of the plant, to conserve moisture and ease weeding.*

***Erinus alpinus* (Fairy foxglove)** For walls and crevices. Flowers are various pinks and white.
○, E, 2.5–5cm/1–2in tall

Phlox subulata Evergreen mat. Spring-flowering. Many different forms, any colour except yellow. ○, E, 10 × 30–60cm/4in × 1–2ft

Phuopsis stylosa Forms a shaggy bright green mat massed with pink flowers all summer.
○, 30 × 45cm/1 × 1½ft

***Acaena* 'Blue Haze'** Spreading mats of steel-blue leaflets and sticky dark red burr heads in summer.
E, 10 × 60cm/4in × 2ft

Cotoneaster congestus Small white flowers in spring, large red berries.
E, mat-forming

***Trifolium repens* 'Purpurascens'** Purple-leaved form of the common clover. ○, mat-forming

Ajuga reptans There are many forms with different coloured leaves.
15 × 45cm/6in × 1½ft

***Sedum spurium* 'Dragon's Blood'** A showy stonecrop. Mat-forming. ○, semi-E, 10 × 45cm/4in × 1½ft

◆ *Late flowering sedums such as this attract butterflies.*

EVERGREENS *and* SMALL TREES

EVERGREENS AND SMALL TREES provide a long term shape to a patio, giving a quiet background to spring, summer colour and some interest in the winter. Unless planted in containers, they are fairly permanent features and should be chosen with care.

Magnolia stellata One of the best dwarf shrubby trees. Flowers, white, scented, mid-spring. 2.4 × 2.4m/8 × 8ft

***Thuja occidentalis* 'Rheingold'** Conifers come in many different forms and shapes. Some, like *Thuja orientalis* 'Rosedalis', change colour with the seasons, green in spring, purple in winter. E, 1m × 60cm/3 × 2ft

◆ *Check that the conifer you choose is dwarf.*

***Buxus sempervirens* (Box)** This tough evergreen shrub can be used for topiary and has many variegated forms. E, 2.7 × 2.7m/9 × 9ft

◆ *Here the box has been trimmed to form balls in tubs.*

EVERGREENS *and* SMALL TREES

***Garrya elliptica* (Tassel bush)** A quick-growing, bushy shrub with long 20cm/8in catkins in winter. Does well on a shady wall. Popular with flower arrangers.
E, 4 × 3m/12 × 10ft

***Choisya ternata* (Mexican orange blossom)** Appreciates a sheltered sunny position. Flowers, white, mainly in spring. The glossy leaves are aromatic when crushed. E, 2 × 2.4m/6 × 8ft

◆ *'Aztec Pearl' and 'Sundance' are attractive varieties of choisya.*

21

EVERGREENS *and* SMALL TREES

WHEN SPACE IS RESTRICTED, permanent larger plants must be chosen with care to provide more than one season of interest. Take into account a combination of foliage, flower, fruit, autumn colour and bark.

For permanent plantings choose plants which are hardy in your area.

Before planting, place the plants in position and check from various angles that they are in the best positions.

Cotoneaster White flowers and colourful fruits. Cotoneasters come in many shapes and sizes from prostrate to weeping standards.

***Camellia* 'Frau Minna Seidel'** ('Otome' 'Pink Perfection') Early flowers. Shelter from early morning sun.
◑, E, 2 × 2m/6 × 6ft

***Cistus* 'Elma'** Papery flowers open in the morning and fall in the evening, more appearing each day in summer.
○, E, 1.2 × 1.2m/4 × 4ft

Daphne tangutica Slow growing, easy. Flowers in early summer. Red berries.
E, 1 × 1 m/3 × 3 ft

◆ *Many daphnes are renowned for the scent of their flowers.*

Ballota pseudodictamnus A much branched shrub, with soft foliage and bobble 'flowers' in summer.
E, 45 × 60cm/1½ × 2ft

Fabiana imbricata violacea Heathlike appearance when young, spreading with age. Prefers a light soil.
◑, E, 2.2 × 2m/7 × 6ft

Cytisus praecox 'Allgold' A bushy broom with arching branches, grey-green leaves and rich yellow flowers in spring. ○, 1.5 × 2m/5 × 6ft

Artemisia 'Powis Castle' Aromatic silver filigree foliage contrasts with bright summer colours. E, 60 × 60cm/2 × 2ft

Hypericum olympicum Small shrub with grey-green leaves and golden yellow flowers in summer. ○, 30 × 30cm/1 × 1ft

Laurus nobilis (Sweet bay) Often trimmed to make a topiary ball. Needs shelter. ○, E, 6 × 6m/20 × 20ft

Malus × moerlandsii 'Profusion' The modern varieties of crab apple have attractive features in most seasons with flowers, fruit and autumn leaf colour. 6 × 4m/20 × 13ft

Picea glauca 'Albertiana Conica' Slowly grows into a dense cone with fine, grass green foliage. E, 1m × 45cm/ 3 × 1½ft in ten years

Lonicera nitida 'Baggesen's Gold' Small-leaved evergreen. Keeps its colour well in winter. ○, 1.5 × 2m/5 × 6ft

Erica arborea alpina Compact tree heath with plumes of tiny white flower bells in winter/spring. E, 1.2m/4ft height and spread

PLANTS *for* a HOT TERRACE

THE HOT TERRACE is ideal, providing the drainage is good, for Mediterranean plants and sun lovers. Plants with leaves that are woolly, waxy, silver or narrow and small tolerate drought most readily, but should never be allowed to dry out.

Gazania makes a super display in summer sun with its bright colours and silver leaves. Needs protection from frost but can be overwintered as cuttings.

There are many helianthemums and pinks from which to choose. Propagate by cuttings after flowering.

Many plants will have a prolonged flowering season if dead-headed regularly, especially helianthemums and mesembryanthemums.

Armeria maritima (Thrift) Forms a neat hump, enjoying sun and wind. Flowers can be white, pink or red. 7.5 × 15cm/3 × 6in

Convolvulus cneorum Glistening silver-green leaves, flowering all summer. Not fully hardy. E, 60 × 60cm/2 × 2ft

Dianthus 'Waithman's Beauty' A neat, ground-hugging pink, appreciating good drainage and lime in the soil. E, 10 × 15cm/ 4 × 6in

Linum narbonense 'Heavenly Blue' A hardy plant with grey-green leaves and abundant flowers. 40 × 30cm/16 × 12in

Helianthemum (Rock rose) Makes mounds of evergreen foliage topped with bright flowers. E, 15 × 60cm/6in × 2ft

Mesembryanthemum (Livingstone daisy) Succulent leaves. Bright flowers open in sun. 15 × 15cm/6 × 6in

Triteleia laxa Californian bulb. Loose, many-headed blue-purple flowers in summer. Best near a warm wall. 60cm/2ft

EVEN THOUGH YOUR PLANTS ARE DROUGHT-TOLERANT they will need water, especially until they are established. It is better to soak the plants thoroughly once a week than to water a little each day, which encourages surface-rooting.

Carpenteria californica Bushy shrub with glossy leaves. Single anemone-shaped flowers. Sunny wall. E, 3 × 2m/10 × 6ft

Hibiscus Beautiful tropical-looking blooms and shiny green leaves. Suffers bud-drop if too dry at the roots. 2 × 1.2m/6 × 4ft

Genista lydia Arching or prostrate grey-green branches, linear leaves and bright yellow flowers. 75cm × 2m/2½ × 6ft

Buddleja alternifolia Pretty bush with narrow pale leaves on arching stems. Good as a standard. 3.5 × 4.5m/12 × 15ft

Cordyline australis 'Atropurpurea' Slow-growing tender plant. E, 7.5 × 2.4m/25 × 8ft

◆ *This New Zealand cabbage palm bears plumes of fragrant flowers when 8–10 years old.*

25

PLANTS *for* a HOT TERRACE

COLOUR IS VERY MUCH A MATTER OF INDIVIDUAL TASTE, but, if you fancy a change from red and shocking pink, this beautiful cistus illustrated opposite in dazzling white with the blue of the ceanothus, set off by the silver and grey foliage plants, produces a bright but cooler effect.

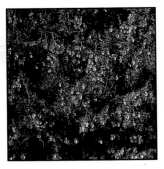

Rosmarinus officinalis (**Rosemary**) Evergreen, aromatic shrub with attractive spring flowers usually in shades of blue, but white and pink varieties are available, as are prostrate and upright forms.

These shrubs prefer poorer soils and, if overfed, are more susceptible to frost damage.

Prune evergreen ceanothus, if required, after flowering; and deciduous, autumn-flowering ones, hard as they come into growth.

Ceanothus impressus A vigorous evergreen shrub with deep green glossy leaves and many clusters of flowers in early spring. Californian 'lilacs' are not the hardiest of shrubs, but grow so well on a wall that they are worth risking. E, $3 \times 3m/10 \times 10ft$

Lavandula (**Lavender**) An indispensable fragrant shrub that is the source of lavender oil. There are many types, some with white or pink flowers, others with leaves that vary from apple green to silver. Attractive to bees and butterflies. E, 30cm–1.2m/ 1–4ft height and spread

Plants *for* a Shady Terrace

IN A SHADY POSITION foliage assumes great importance, as woodland plants tend to be less floriferous and brightly coloured than sun lovers. Plants with large lush leaves that wilt and scorch in sun and wind will thrive in moist shade. Colour is an important consideration. White and gold are the most dramatic colours in shade. Variegated foliage will provide pools of light against green backgrounds.

***Aucuba japonica* 'Variegata'**
Few shrubs tolerate shade as well as aucubas. A variegated form will brighten any dark corner. E, 3 × 2 m/10 × 6 ft

***Camellia* 'Inspiration'**
Camellias thrive best in light, acid soils enriched with leaf mould to help retain moisture. They prefer dappled shade, or a cool wall. ◑, E, 3 × 2m/ 10 × 6ft

Rhododendrons come in all shapes and sizes. Flower colours are from near blue to red, pink, white and yellow. Some are scented.

Use spring bulbs such as bluebells, wood anemones and dog's tooth violets to fill gaps.

The variegated forms of *Vinca minor* maintain their foliage colour throughout the year.

***Rhododendron* 'Praecox'**
Rosy mauve flowers early in the year; best protected from frost by overhead tree canopy. All rhododendrons need acid soil. ◑, E, 1.2–2 × 1.2–2m/4–6 × 4–6ft

◆ *Winter aconites,* Eranthis hyemalis, *are very effective planted around rhododendrons.*

Hydrangeas are excellent shrubs for mid and late summer in light shade and moisture retentive soils. The dying flower heads turn an attractive colour and should not be pruned away until growth starts in the spring. Flower colour can be affected by the acidity/alkalinity of the soil.

Hydrangea **serrata 'Grayswood'** Blue fertile flowers surrounded by large white ray florets which mature to crimson. A beautiful hybrid of lax habit, needing light shade. 1.2 × 1.2m/4 × 4ft

PLANTS *for* a SHADY TERRACE

Cotoneaster horizontalis
Deciduous shrub with herringbone branches. Pink flowers followed by red berries. 60cm × 2m/ 2 × 6ft, taller against a wall

Hedera helix 'Parsley Crested' Attractive ivy which will cling to most surfaces and eventually cover a large area, in sun or shade.

Parthenocissus henryana Self-clinging climber. Variegated leaves, best in shade, brilliant red in autumn. 10m/30ft height

Fatsia japonica This is grown for its handsome evergreen foliage and dramatic white flowers in autumn. 3 × 3m/10 × 10ft

Pernettya (Gaultheria) mucronata Lime-hating. Berries in autumn, colour dependent on variety. E, 1.2m × 60cm/4 × 2ft

Skimmia japonica Fragrant flowers in spring followed by red berries (male and female plants required). E, 1.2 × 2m/4 × 6ft

Mahonia aquifolium (Oregon grape) Suckering shrub, fragrant yellow flowers in spring, blue-black berries. E, 1.2 × 2m/4 × 6ft

Convallaria majalis (Lily of the valley) Arching stems carry sweet smelling flowers in early spring. 15 × 60cm/6in × 2ft

Bergenia cordifolia A tough plant with shiny, leathery leaves. Pink early-spring flowers. E, 30 × 60cm/ 1 × 2ft

Asplenium scolopendrium (Hart's tongue fern) for walls. Adiantum ferns for damp; polystichums for dry shade.

FEW PLANTS GROW WELL IN COMPLETE SHADE. Deciduous trees and shrubs allow more light in winter, providing better conditions for spring bulbs and herbaceous plants, such as hellebores and pulsatillas, which flower early in the year.

Polygonatum × hybridum
Solomon's seal with attractive arching stems and white flowers in early summer. 1m × 30cm/3 × 1ft

Cyclamen hederifolium
Flowers from late summer into winter. The marbled leaves persist until spring. 7.5 × 30cm/3in × 1ft

Primula vulgaris There are very many double forms of the primrose. 15 × 30cm/6in × 1ft

Divide double primroses when they start to get congested, about every three years.

Sawfly larvae will eat polygonatum leaves in midsummer. Spray insecticide or pick them off.

BEDDING

Shady areas tend to lack brightness, and bedding plants and bulbs will supply more colour. Use daffodils, winter aconites and hyacinths for spring, impatiens (*right*) for summer and, later, winter pansies.

◆ *Digitalis purpurea (foxgloves) will brighten dark areas. They are biennials, flowering in their second year.*

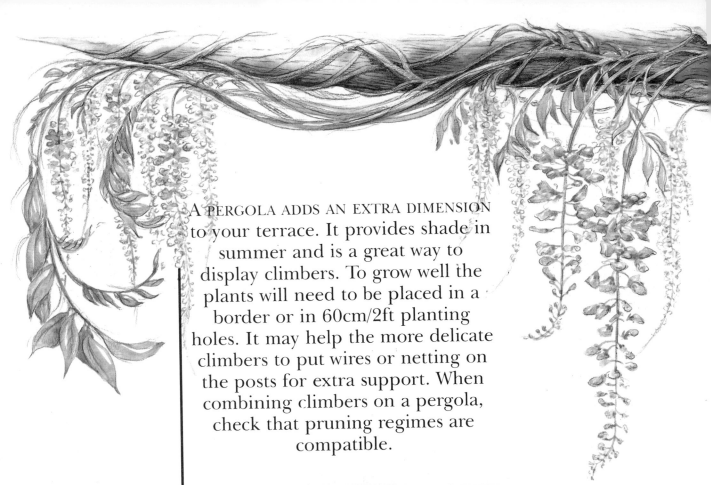

A PERGOLA ADDS AN EXTRA DIMENSION to your terrace. It provides shade in summer and is a great way to display climbers. To grow well the plants will need to be placed in a border or in 60cm/2ft planting holes. It may help the more delicate climbers to put wires or netting on the posts for extra support. When combining climbers on a pergola, check that pruning regimes are compatible.

CLIMBERS *for* PERGOLAS

Clematis **'Gipsy Queen'** A vigorous grower with a three-month flowering season. The flowers are 15cm/6in in diameter and combine well with a pink rose. 3.5–6m/12–20ft

◆ *Clematis prefer cool root runs, so plant on the shady side of the post.*

Wisteria The classic spring flower for a pergola, but it needs to be trained and pruned. Halve and tie in the new growth in summer. In winter halve the extension shoots again and prune side shoots to three buds.

Rosa **'Madame Grégoire Staechelin'** A vigorous climber with a profusion of double, scented flowers in early summer. Prefers some shade. 3.5–6m/12–20ft

◆ *This rose makes an ideal support for a late-flowering clematis.*

2. POTS AND HANGING BASKETS

Pots and containers have three great virtues: they can be moved anywhere, you can give plants the conditions they need and you can easily change them.

CHOOSING POTS

CONTAINERS COME IN ALL SHAPES AND SIZES. Large pots are easier to maintain as they do not dry out as quickly as small ones. All pots must have drainage holes. Terracotta is the traditional material for ornamental pots, but make sure that your pot will withstand frost if it is left outside in winter.

STRAWBERRY POT
Use a strong compost and take care to leave sufficient room to water without washing the soil away.

HERB POT
Watering is a problem with this type of container. A pipe with holes in it, placed centrally, will help.

PLASTIC POT
These come in many shapes and sizes, are relatively cheap and easy to handle. They are not porous and therefore do not dry out as quickly as terracotta.

WALL POT
Be sure the fixings are strong enough for the combined weight of pot, wet compost and plants.

RECONSTITUTED STONE
These can be aged with diluted cow manure or liquid fertilizer, to encourage algae.

Wooden tubs and barrels make good containers but may need some maintenance to prevent rotting.

Concrete containers are cheap but very heavy – they do not blow over easily!

GLAZED POT AND SAUCER
In wet weather, check that the saucer is not full of water.

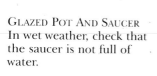

Siting Containers

Colour co-ordinated pots. Many different plants grouped together can look something of a hotch-potch but care with the choice of shape and colour makes this an attractive feature.

◆ *Unity is added to the group by using pots of the same material.*

Phormium* (New Zealand flax) and *Aruncus dioicus
This shows how effective a pot can be when temporarily placed by a border with the plants complementing each other. The bronze form of phormium shows up well against the cream background.

Aeonium in a pot 'playing a role' in a gravel bed. Plants normally confined to the greenhouse can be used in summer to give a dramatic impact in the garden.

◆ *Many house and greenhouse plants appreciate a summer out of doors.*

CONTAINERS CAN ENLIVEN DULL CORNERS, fill gaps in borders, hide manhole covers, distract the eye from ugly buildings, make herb gardens by the kitchen door or hold scented plants near a seat. They are movable gardens and are also more easily renewed than the plantings of beds and borders.

Containers need to be in scale with their surroundings. This large, handsome pot provides the focus of attention for the terraced area. It would be satisfactory, even if not planted.

Containers can be used to decorate steps, larger free-standing pots at the bottom and smaller ones on the steps. Use drought-resistant plants so the steps are not always wet. Scented plants are pleasant to brush past.

Tulipa **'Madame Lefeber'** Tulips grow well in pots for a season, making a good display in spring, especially when given a background emphasizing their colour.

PLANTING
a
CONTAINER

Do not leave air pockets around the plant's roots – they do not grow well in air.

Repot before winter, so that the plant is growing strongly before the cold weather.

Shade for a few days after repotting in hot weather, to give the plant time to re-establish.

1. The base of a clay pot will require 'crocking' – pieces of broken pot put in to cover the drainage hole(s) and prevent soil loss. The holes in plastic pots are generally smaller and do not need crocks.

2. Choose a pot larger, but not too much so, than the root ball. Scrape some of the old top layer of compost off the root ball and carefully tease out some roots.

3. Next choose the appropriate compost for your plant, lime-free, or quick-draining, or with added water-retaining granules.

4. Part fill the pot, leaving room for the root ball. Fill round the plant, nearly to the rim, firming carefully.

POTTING ON

Plants will suffer in pots if they outgrow them. Replant perennials in fresh compost in a larger container. They can alternatively be divided or you can trim the roots of shrubby forms by about a quarter.

PLANT YOUR BULBS IN AUTUMN for spring flowering. If your winters are very cold, store the containers in a shed or garage, or protect with sacking or bubble polythene. Many bulbs will rot if frozen solid and the soil in pots is much more vulnerable to freezing than in the open ground.

PLANTING
a
CONTAINER

Spring Pots. The variegated ivy stands out brightly against the hedge, the tulips and primrose adding a welcome splash of colour.

◆ *The effectiveness of the group is increased by the differing heights of the pots.*

PLANTS *for* SUN

ANNUALS AND SOFT PERENNIALS provide many of the plants suitable for pots on sunny patios. If a lot are required this can be an expensive enterprise. Seeds can be germinated on well-lit window-sills and grown on in small frames outside. Cuttings from perennials can be overwintered on window-sills and rapidly grow to good-sized plants in a frame or greenhouse.

Rosa **'Sweet Dream'** Patio roses need a fertile soil, sun, good drainage, dead-heading and a light pruning in spring. 20 × 30cm/8in × 1ft

◆ *Roses do best without other plants growing through them.*

Schizanthus Attractive annuals with variously coloured flowers. May need some support. Pinch the growing tips of young plants to encourage bushiness.
60 × 30cm/2 × 1ft

Containers carefully chosen, grouped together and packed with plants, make a spectacular display. The colour of the silver **helichrysum** and pale blue **lobelia** complement each other and set off the shocking pink **pelargonium**. The blue *Convolvulus sabatius* shows up well with the glistening white **marguerite**. Trailing plants help to bind the design together.

PLANTS *for* SUN

PLANTS GROWN IN POTS WILL NEED REGULAR FEEDING if they are to give a good display throughout the summer. A liquid feed high in potash is required for flower production and nitrogen for foliage. During the flowering season it is sensible to feed plants at least once a week.

Brugmansia (Angel's trumpet, Datura) Fragrant. Tender. Water well.
2 × 2.4m/6 × 8ft

◆ *Daturas are poisonous, especially the flowers and fruit. Handle with care.*

Heliotropium × hybridum **(Cherry pie)** Corymbs of scented flowers all summer. Not hardy.
30 × 45cm/1 × 1½ft

Felicia amelloides **(Blue marguerite)** Not hardy, so collect seeds or take cuttings.
45 × 30cm/1½ × 1ft

Agave americana **(Century plant)** Succulent with sword leaves, tipped with spines. Dangerous to children. Not hardy. 1 × 1m/3 × 3ft

Plumbago capensis A beautiful container shrub, flowering all summer, but needs to be frost free.
1.5m × 60cm/5 × 2ft

Argyranthemum White, pink or yellow double or single flowers. Dead-head regularly. Tender. 60 × 45cm/2 × 1½ft

Abutilon × hybridum Makes a splendid pot plant but needs to winter frost-free. Prune in early spring. 1m × 60cm/3 × 2ft

Callistemon rigidus (Bottle brush) Will need some frost protection in all but the mildest areas. 1 × 1.2m/ 3 × 4ft

Begonia Pendulous begonias, trained as standards, make very effective pot plants. 60cm × 1m/2 × 3ft

Echeveria Makes an interesting container plant for the patio or terrace. Needs little water. Not hardy. 7.5 × 15cm/3 × 6in

Gazania These daisy flowers open and close with the sun. 23 × 23cm/9 × 9in

Narcissus 'Tête à Tête' One of the best multi-headed dwarf daffodils. Feed in spring and repot each summer. 23cm/9in

The violas, if the winter is not too hard, will brighten this display until the tulips flower.

Lilium 'Connecticut King' Lilies grow well in pots. Use good compost and plant deeply. 75cm/2½ft tall

PLANTS *for* SUN

The modern varieties of **Regal pelargoniums** are very free-flowering, especially if fed and dead-headed regularly. 60 × 30cm/2 × 1ft

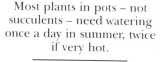

Most plants in pots – not succulents – need watering once a day in summer, twice if very hot.

It is better to water early or late, rather than when the sun is hottest.

Water-retaining granules can be mixed with the compost at planting to reduce drying out.

PLANTS *for* PART SHADE

IT IS IMPORTANT TO CHOOSE PLANTS FOR SHADE that are adapted, like woodlanders, to live in low-light conditions. Those preferring sun will grow lank, with pale leaves and few flowers, if grown in shade.

Hydrangea macrophylla **'Madame Emile Mouillère'** A beautiful, but tender, hydrangea with large white flowers which become tinted pink later in the season. Needs semi-shade and a moist soil. 1.2 × 2m/4 × 6ft

There are many varieties of **Hosta**, from large plants, suitable for a barrel, to plants for a small pot. Silver or gold variegations look good in the shade.

◆ *Watch out for slugs in the early spring when the leaves are unfurling.*

Rhododendron flavidum 'Album' Small rhododendron suitable for pot culture. Prune after flowering. E, 60cm × 1m/ 2 × 3ft

◆ *Rhododendrons need a lime-free compost and must not dry out.*

Primula obconica Pink, red-purple or blue-purple flowers in early spring. Usually grown as an annual. The light green leaves are hairy and cause an allergic reaction in some people's skins. 45 × 20cm/ 1½ft × 8in

Euonymus fortunei Makes an effective standard. E, 4.5 × 1.5m/15 × 5ft unpruned

◆ *There are many variegated varieties available.*

PLANTS *for* PART SHADE

Begonia semperflorens 'Kalinka Rose' Tuberous begonias are very versatile and will grow in sun or semi-shade.
60cm × 1m/2 × 3ft

Pieris japonica Evergreen shrub, with red young shoots and racemes of white flowers in spring.
E, 3 × 3m/10 × 10ft

◆ *Pieris needs a lime-free soil and must not dry out.*

Hosta 'Halcyon' Blue textured leaves and lilac flowers in midsummer.
60 × 60cm/2 × 2ft

Eucomis bicolor (Pineapple plant) A spectacular bulb with long-lasting flowers in midsummer and attractive seed capsules. 45cm/1½ft

Polystichum setiferum 'Acutilobum' (Soft shield fern) The attractive fronds retain their colour all winter. 1 × 1m/3 × 3ft

Lilium regale Beautiful fragrant summer-flowering lily. Stem rooting, so plant deeply. 1.2–2m/4–6ft tall

Lilium 'Pink Perfection' A tall hybrid of *L. regale* which bears large scented trumpets. 1.2m/4ft or more

PLANTS IN POTS IN SEMI-SHADE do not need as much water as those in full sun, but more care is needed removing dead flowers and foliage to prevent the spread of moulds and other diseases.

Acer palmatum dissectum Beautiful cut leaves and superb autumn colour. 4.5 × 2.4m/15 × 8ft eventually

◆ *These deciduous trees need protection from wind and sun.*

Cassiope 'Muirhead' Dwarf heath-like shrub with white bell flowers in spring. For lime-free soil. E, 10 × 30cm/4 × 12in

Tradescantia virginiana 'Purple Dome' A hardy plant, flowering from early summer to autumn. 60 × 45cm/2 × 1½ft

Magnificent specimens of **Fuchsia 'Checkerboard'** and *F.* **'Orange Mirage'** raised on a plinth.

◆ *A high-phosphate feed in summer helps flowering.*

TUBS *and* BARRELS

MOST TUBS AND BARRELS used in the garden are wooden. These should be treated on the inside so that the wood does not rot, either with a preserving fluid or by briefly burning the inside of the barrel to produce a thin protective layer of charcoal.

Trachycarpus fortunei (Chusan palm) Needs shelter from cold winds. E, 2–3m/6–10ft high

◆ *Pot up offsets to make new plants.*

This copper tub makes a splendid centrepiece to this circle of roof tiles and granite sets.

◆ *The apricot red and yellow shades tone well with the blue-green of the copper.*

Ivy-leaved pelargoniums achieve great height, when carefully staked, and flower all summer. The silver helichrysum cools the pink very effectively.

◆ *This barrel is well framed by the dark green background.*

Evergreens including a box
ball around a summer
planting of marguerites.

Camellia **'Anticipation'** Camellias
make excellent shrubs for a large
container of the acid, humus-rich
soil they relish. With the aid of
rollers, the barrel may be moved
from its prominent flowering
position and placed so that it
retreats into the background for
the rest of the year.

SINKS *and* TROUGHS

To minimise back strain, put your trough in its final position before filling it with compost.

Keep your trough off the ground with bricks or slate for good drainage.

New troughs 'age' better in the shade.

A combination of troughs and pots makes an attractive group in the corner of a patio. The pots can be changed to prolong the flowering season.

◆ *This is a good way to combine plants with different growing requirements.*

Before filling the trough with compost, cover the drainage holes with crocks.

Top dress the compost with gravel to keep the plants' necks dry to help prevent rotting.

This handsome stone trough makes a good home for alpine sedums.

◆ *Complementary plantings beneath unite the trough with its surroundings.*

This attractive trough of pansies and lobelia will give a long display if fed and dead-headed.

◆ *In front, both flowers and seed-heads are beautiful.*

SINKS AND TROUGHS are most commonly used for small alpine plants. Attractive, semi-permanent miniature gardens can be created in this way, but narrow troughs can also be planted like window boxes, the display changing with the seasons.

The trough shown opposite is used here for a splendid spring effect. Again the planting has been kept unfussy and simple, just two: grape hyacinths (muscari) and double daisies (*Bellis perennis*).

◆ *The spires of the muscari contrast well with the saucer-flowers of the daisies.*

SINKS *and* TROUGHS

Stone trough on legs with white petunias rising above blue lobelia.

Another elegant trough with nemesias making a brilliant display.

Trailing silver helichrysum, pelargoniums and fuchsias in another raised trough.

Lewisia cotyledon hybrids flowering in a stone alpine trough in summer.

◆ *Lewisias are best kept in an alpine house in winter to prevent rot from wet; or outside, grow them on their sides in a wall.*

Foliage plants (begonias and fern) with the hardy annual hare's tail grass (*Lagurus ovatus*). An original planting.

Beautiful old trough with sempervivums and a little bush of *Alyssum spinosum roseum*.

HYPERTUFA

STONE TROUGHS ARE INCREASINGLY RARE and also expensive. An alternative is to make a hypertufa trough. Hypertufa is a very versatile material and can look good quite quickly. When aged it can be hard to distinguish from stone.

1. Hypertufa is made from one part each of cement, dry sharp, or concreting, sand and finely sieved peat or coco fibre. PVA bonding agent will give strength and flowability. Mix and add water, mixing until the compound just flows.

2. Find two boxes to give walls 4–5cm/ 1½–2in thick. Put the base layer in the larger box and make two drainage holes. Tamp. Place the second box centrally on the base. Larger troughs need wire reinforcement for the base and sides.

3. Support the sides of the outer box and fill the inner box with sand, then continue filling the sides. Tamp. Cover with wet fabric and leave for 36 hours. Carefully remove fabric and boxes.

4. Shape with old knives and a stiff brush. Open up drain holes. Replace wet fabric and leave to set for 2 or 3 days, when it will be strong enough to move. Plant one week later.

UNUSUAL CONTAINERS

This elegant lead urn, and the granite sets surrounding it, would flatter any planting.

Home-made Water Garden. A wooden container with a liner makes an attractively planted water garden.

These chimney pots make an interesting group with the wall pots. They also look good with hanging plants.

A large glazed jar with its agave, and the trellis work, gives an exotic air to a patio.

These alpines and dwarf conifers are growing very happily in this old iron bath and make a very satisfying group with the iron pot spilling its red rock rose onto the gravel.

◆ *The imaginative placing of the iron pot distinguishes this grouping.*

A PLANT-CONTAINER CAN BE ANYTHING that holds compost from a plastic ice-cream tub to a lead cistern. All that is required is some growing medium and drainage holes. Pots can be painted, or clad in wood for effect.

This barrow, with its load of startling white marguerites (argyranthemums), dangling pink pelargoniums and blue lobelia, is cleverly placed in front of a yew hedge which provides an ideal background.

◆ *Many artefacts can be put to decorative use in the garden.*

Forest trees can be grown in small containers, if carefully watered and pruned. Their branches may be wired to achieve the desired shape.

A painted barrow is given its own cobbled area to form a novel focal point in the garden.

There are still old washhouse coppers in rural areas which can be put to good use as planters, preferably with drainage holes in the base.

HANGING BASKETS PROVIDE additional space for plants, add height to your displays and can be placed at different levels to enliven a boring wall. They can be hung on any strong structure to make a display in the middle of your patio.

The bright colours in this basket are beautifully set off by the grey stone wall.

◆ *The trailing variegated glechoma (ground ivy) links the basket to the window box.*

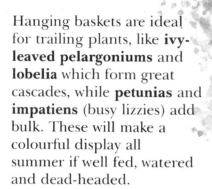

Hanging baskets are ideal for trailing plants, like **ivy-leaved pelargoniums** and **lobelia** which form great cascades, while **petunias** and **impatiens** (busy lizzies) add bulk. These will make a colourful display all summer if well fed, watered and dead-headed.

These twin baskets benefit from lots of blue to make a contrast to the red bricks.

◆ *Silver foliage also looks good against bricks.*

PLANTING *a* BASKET

MOISTURE GRANULES

Watering is a big problem with hanging baskets, but these granules will help if they are added to the planting compost when you make up the basket.

The picture below shows the same granules twenty minutes after water has been added to them. They have absorbed it and the basket will enjoy damp conditions as the granules gradually release their moisture.

If your basket does dry out, get it down and stand it in water for a couple of hours.

CHOOSE AS LARGE A BASKET as the situation allows; larger baskets dry out less quickly than smaller ones. A liner is required to hold in the planting compost and moisture. There are various types available, including the traditional sphagnum moss, but here we show how to plant up a basket using a simple polythene liner.

1. The aim is to plant the basket sufficiently densely that the liner is not visible, just a complete sphere of flowers. Before filling the basket with soil, cut holes in the liner around the sides.
2. Gradually fill the basket with planting compost, moisture granules and fertilizer (if this is not already present in the compost), putting plants through the holes you have made as the basket fills up.

3. Cut off any spare liner. Squeeze in a good number of plants to produce a well covered basket and then water thoroughly. It will take three or four weeks for the plants to develop sufficiently to cover the basket. During this time it may be best to keep the basket in an easily accessible, sheltered place for watering before hanging it in its final location.

Your basket will do best in a position sheltered from wind. It will need a strong bracket, firmly fixed.

For ease of maintenance and watering, pulleys are available to enable the basket to be lowered.

In dry, hot weather your basket will need watering twice a day. Automatic watering systems are available.

If the basket looks tired in midsummer use a high nitrogen liquid feed for a fortnight.

SITING HANGING BASKETS

HANGING BASKETS will look best in sheltered positions as wind causes them to dry out quickly and breaks brittle foliage. If they are placed too high, watering can be a problem. Their main function is as decoration and they should be sited where they can be seen to best advantage.

Baskets hanging from a pergola, a covered terrace and at the entrance to a house – three positions where they will be best appreciated.

◆ *Scented plants would be particularly successful on a pergola.*

PLANTS FOR HANGING BASKETS need to be tough to survive in their exposed environment. Trailing plants and those which produce a mass of blooms on short stems to cover the basket with foliage and flowers are a better choice than those with tall rigid stems.

PLANTS *for* BASKETS

Helichrysum petiolare An indispensable plant for hanging baskets. The cool silver foliage sets off bright colours and hangs gracefully.

Ivies do well in semi-shade or in a winter display and trail daintily.

A much rounder effect is gained by using only one type of plant. In a mild winter, these pansies will flower until spring.

◆ *Even in winter, water will be required, especially in cold windy weather.*

PLANTS *for* BASKETS

Consider the background before choosing the plants.

Petunias in their various shades make a bold splash. Modern varieties are more rain resistant.

This combination of perlargoniums (geraniums), petunias, calceolarias and impatiens (busy lizzies) makes a colourful display.

Diascia vigilis This hardy diascia will grow happily in a hanging basket and, with a little trimming, will look good all summer.

***Fuchsia* 'Miss California'** Trailing fuchsias show themselves to advantage in hanging baskets.

◆ *Fuchsias do well in shade or partial shade.*

Lotus berthelotii This spectacular silver-leaved plant enjoys sun and adds drama to any hanging basket.

Blue lobelia is a very useful foil to reds and pinks, cooling strident shades. Easily raised from seed.

Mimulus (Monkey flower) comes in many shades of red, orange and yellow, sometimes with spots.

Calceolaria prefers a light acid soil in sun or partial shade.

Use baskets with saucers where drips could be a nuisance.

Bidens ferulifolia has bright yellow daisy flowers which flow over the edges of baskets.

Some varieties of patio and ground-cover roses can be grown for a short period in the basket.

Begonia semperflorens Always a tidy plant with red or green foliage and red, pink or white flowers.

◆ *They grow happily in sun or shade.*

Impatiens 'Picotee Swirl' This busy lizzie would brighten any shady corner in summer.

◆ *A basket with one variety can look very effective.*

65

3. WINDOW BOXES

These are of particular value to town gardeners, but country cottages can also be ornamented by a brilliant display at the windows.

WINDOW BOX SYSTEMS

This raised bed, made from bricks, makes a good window box, providing a cool root run and needing less watering than a conventional box.

Check window sills for weight bearing capacity.

Water gently to avoid washing compost onto walls and windows below.

Before buying a window box, check how your windows open!

This window box, with a plastic insert, works well as the wood will rot less quickly, not being in contact with the soil, and the display can be changed easily, when required.

◆ *This system also allows you to dunk the trough in water if it dries out.*

Plastic boxes need little maintenance and are light – an advantage on weak sills.

A hay rack with a liner can look very attractive where sills are narrow.

These wooden boxes, with decorative restraining bars, blend well with the austere window surrounds.

TRY TO CHOOSE A SIMPLE WINDOW BOX in style with your building – a hay rack may look out of place on a modern block, or too ornate a box may dominate your plants. Above all, whatever you choose must be secure and able to bear the weight of soil and plants.

A simple restraining bar can be very effective, allowing the use of plants in pots which can be changed through the seasons to maintain the display.

◆ *Take care that top-heavy plants cannot fall over the bar.*

A Spring Display

WINTER DISPLAYS OF PANSIES and evergreens can easily be changed to spring displays with the help of daffodils, tulips or hyacinths to give extra colour and stronger shapes and to contrast with the existing plants.

This combination of clipped boxes, ivies and skimmias will have provided interest all winter and the scented flowers of the skimmias now herald spring.

Compact wallflowers can add scent as well as colour.

Bulbs grown in pots are useful for filling gaps.

These rich violet pansies and glowing yellow tulips would brighten any dull spring day.

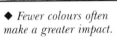 *◆ Fewer colours often make a greater impact.*

The daffodils provide a link between the hay rack and the small bed, extending the colour across the whole elevation.

The modern varieties of winter pansies have a long flowering season and, in mild winters, flower straight through, with the best flush in the spring.

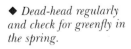 *◆ Dead-head regularly and check for greenfly in the spring.*

This display is essentially short term, but magnificent while it lasts and is suitable for boxes with interchangeable liners. The **trailing ivy** clothes the box and balances the height of the **tulips** and **hyacinths**. The tulips' strong shape cuts through the frothy blue **forget-me-nots** while the hyacinths' rich fragrance can drift into the house through an open window.

SUMMER BLOOMS

NOW IS THE TIME FOR EXTRAVAGANT GROWTH and vibrant colours. A little planning will give a dramatic display which, with a little maintenance (feeding, dead-heading and watering), will last well into autumn.

The shocking pink petunias, red ivy-leaved pelargoniums (geraniums) combined with the dashing orange shades of the nemesia and cooled by the dark blue white-eyed lobelia, make a stunning display.

◆ *The white walls and curtains make a perfect cool background.*

The large variety of plants in this window box, with strongly differing shapes and colours, accentuates the vertical line of the split blinds behind.

◆ *This sort of effect can also be achieved by using separate pots.*

***Pelargonium* 'Roller's Pioneer'** Ivy-leaved pelargoniums are excellent in containers, having succulent, drought-resistant leaves. They will flower in cascades until the frosts, or all winter in warmth.

The ivy on the wall surrounding this window box, with its pelargoniums (geraniums) and petunias, gives a charming cottagey effect, as if it all grew out of the wall unaided.

◆ *The ivy may be kept in bounds by pruning.*

Use plants with similar food and water requirements together to ease maintenance.

When you buy plants, choose the sturdier young plants showing buds rather than those that are lanky and flowering.

Always plant something scented in your displays.

This window box of begonias, petunias, dahlia, impatiens and lobelia adds height to the collection of plants beneath. The use of similar colours unifies the container.

◆ *Reds look well against subdued backgrounds.*

SUMMER BLOOMS

Watering is best done in the cool of the evening, to reduce evaporation loss.

Gazania Sun-loving cream and yellow flowers well set off by bright silver foliage.

Petunia These are well suited to a sunny position but are less happy in a rainy season. A mainstay of most window boxes.

The petunias, verbena and pelargoniums, plants with similar requirements, combine very well to give a good display.

The zonal pelargoniums are well matched with the petunias, falling forwards and flowing into the variegated ground ivy, carrying the colour down the wall.

Zonal pelargoniums are strongly growing, upright plants and can make a fine display on their own.

SUMMER BLOOMS

The white fuchsia and the apricot and yellow argyranthemums (marguerites) are highlighted by the bright blue lobelia, creating a lovely effect against the warm brick wall.

A display of trailing pelargoniums giving continuous colour and good, disease-resistant foliage.

Impatiens (busy lizzies) have a tidy habit, flower continuously and are happy in shade.

Never give liquid feeds to a dry container.

Pelargoniums are commonly called geraniums.

Tuberous begonias are available in many colours and, with their shining foliage, give a tropical air.

The pendulous begonias add a luxuriant feel with their shiny pointed leaves and lush satiny flowers glowing against the blue-mauve of the zonal pelargonium.

AUTUMN *and* WINTER

UNLESS YOU LIVE IN A FROST-FREE ZONE, most of your summer and autumn plants will be dead by mid-winter, but it is not necessary for your window box to be full of depressing flowerless sticks all winter. There are many hardy evergreens which will brighten this season, with a minimum of maintenance, some of which will then come into flower in spring.

The variegated hebe is balanced by the ivy, the gold and cream set off by the black window box.

◆ *Check that the compost is not too dry at regular intervals.*

The griselinia adds height and substance to this arrangement.

◆ *These shrubs can be kept for several winters.*

This is an effective arrangement of silver and gold foliage with the splash of red berries.

◆ *An occasional trim will keep the little shrubs smart.*

This combination of evergreens makes a satisfying display. The **heathers** will flower in late winter and set off the clipped **boxes** which give shape and height. The **ivies** trail, softening the edges and countering the rigid shapes of the boxes and heathers. Some summer-flowering heathers change colour in winter to bright reds and golds and can therefore be valuable for their winter foliage.

THE COTTAGE GARDEN

(*Above*) A close planting of forget-me-nots, pansies and the blue *Centaurea montana*.
(*Right*) Quintessential cottage borders with pinks, roses and foxgloves overhanging the path.

THE COTTAGE GARDEN is traditionally a small, densely planted plot, best described as delightful chaotic profusion. It is not too contrived and yet carefully tended, every available niche and space being used. Most of the garden will consist of paths and borders with small patches of grass near the house or beneath fruit trees. The dense borders which are the main characteristic of the cottage garden are planted with tall perennials, shrubs and ground-cover plants, interspersed with self-seeding annuals and biennials. Many of the plants have domestic uses as herbs, fruit, aromatics and bee-nectar plants. Salad plants and vegetables grow in small plots amongst the flowers or in vegetable plots surrounded by borders of herbs and aromatic plants, which deter insect pests from finding their 'host' vegetables.

The true cottage garden was not contrived and most of its space was devoted to food production. Flowers were tucked here and there and arrived through friends or were started from bits taken from the borders of the 'Big House'. Seeds came on boots, by birds and on the wind or were transplanted from hedgerow and meadow. Native plants which had abnormalities such as variegated leaves or white or double flowers were collected in such gardens since early times. Dotted planting, where plants of different characteristics are grown together, is a true feature of cottage gardens. Nowadays a sense of structure can be introduced by a clipped hedge, stone ornament, arch or seat.

HISTORY OF THE COTTAGE GARDEN

There is little written about cottage gardens prior to 1750. A cottager may have been any-

(*Left*) This painting, which dates from the end of the nineteenth century, is by Helen Allingham. Though realistic (note the washing on the line and the ramshackle fence), it exemplifies the ideal cottage in the country, old, pretty, its garden filled with plants.

(*Right*) A dreamy close planting of day-lilies and *Campanula lactiflora*.

one who worked on a big estate but did not live in the 'Big House', including farm workers, gardeners and dairymen or they may have been small farmers or country craftsmen. The medieval cottage garden was probably just a yard with animals, separated into sections by hurdles. One of the sections would be used for growing vegetables and corn, and the sections rotated each year. Farmstead gardens consisted of a small orchard, a turf area and rectangular beds for herbs and vegetables. These yeoman-farmer gardens became the inspiration for the grander small country houses which began to adopt the cottage gar-

den style by the late eighteenth century. Romantic cottage gardens also had features reminiscent of the pleasure gardens of medieval and Tudor manor houses such as topiary, arches, bowers and decorative trelliswork.

By the beginning of the twentieth century, the cottage garden had declined due to an increase in short-term tenancies of cottages and an increase in the urban population. The cottage garden style continued to evolve in the grander country cottages inhabited by relatively wealthy people. Garden writers such as William Robinson and Gertrude Jekyll in the

Features like walls and paths were purely functional in old cottage gardens. Use any existing trees and shrubs, providing they do not obscure your best view nor have been planted too close to the house. A bit of shade in the garden can be useful, providing another kind of habitat for herbaceous plants. Decide where your paths, borders and grass areas will be and whether you need to break the garden into sections or 'rooms' by using trellises, fences and hedges. You may find that your soil varies in different areas of the garden: a dry well-drained patch is ideal for most herbs; a damp area can be transformed into a lush bog garden; and an area of subsoil and rubble can be dug out and made into a feature such as a sunken stone garden or a pond.

Before planting borders, as many weeds as possible should be removed, especially where perennials will be planted. Rotovating is not a good idea for a perennial bed since it chops up weed roots and multiplies them. (In a vegetable patch which is regularly cultivated, the rotovator has its uses.) The borders are now ready to be planted with shrubs, roses, and clumps of perennials.

Well-meaning friends will soon offer you pieces of herbaceous plants. If you see any sign of a perennial weed growing in the clump, throw the whole lot away. It is virtually impossible to completely remove weeds such as ground elder (*Aegopodium podagraria*) once they have grown into another plant. Scatter as many annual seeds as possible amongst your perennials. These will provide you with a show of dense colour for the first year and many will provide a seed bank of self-sown plants for future growing seasons.

late nineteenth century, popularized the more informal and natural approach to gardening. In the 1970s the cottage garden style enjoyed another revival as part of the interest in wildlife and organic gardening. This interest is still gathering momentum.

DESIGN AND PLANNING

Few of us start a garden from scratch but inherit other peoples' mistakes and tastes in gardening. When starting, it is advisable to eradicate fiddly elements such as rockeries and weed-filled walls rather than spend valuable time trying to make them look pleasant.

MANAGEMENT

A friend who has been a cottage gardener for fifty years once told me that one must be prepared to 'waltz plants around the garden'. The random and informal style of cottage gardening results in some being planted in the wrong place. But many chance and happy unplanned plant associations will be discovered. Growing old-fashioned varieties of plants rather than modern hybrids will result in colour tones that tend to harmonize with each other. Making notes of plants that look good next to each other whilst visiting other gardens or looking through books will add to your repertoire of pleasing plantings.

Some gardeners rush to dead-head a plant once its flower is over but seed heads can be very attractive and provide food for seed-eating birds. The advantages of leaving perennial plants uncut through the winter are that the plants are better protected from cold and are not tempted to make growth during a warm spell and they will more readily seed down. They also provide food for birds and over-wintering sites for beneficial insects. Nutrients from the border plants are recycled, which helps maintain soil fertility. Borders can be cut back in early spring and carefully and selectively weeded. Mulching with a light covering of bark, lawn-mowings or leaf mould throughout the growing season, should result in less weeding the following spring. Each year note the plants that are becoming too large or rampant and move them to another site later in the season. The advantage of dense planting which is so characteristic of cottage gardens is that many plants will support each other and the need for staking will be reduced.

Typical cottage plants, lupins and *Rosa* 'Albertine'.

Nepeta, white foxgloves and geraniums form twin borders either side of the path which leads to an open door, encouraging you to walk beyond it.

THE COTTAGE GARDEN TODAY

The revival of interest in the cottage garden corresponds with the awareness of organic cultivation and the value of wildlife gardening. Many insect pests have natural insect predators and a wide range of plants, including wild flowers, in the garden helps to provide nectar and pollen needed at various stages of the predatory insect's life cycle. Trees and shrubs and carefully sited nest-boxes soon attract a variety of birds. The relatively undisturbed habitat of the mixed shrub and perennial border is an ideal habitat for hedgehogs. A small pond will soon be buzzing with aquatic life. Wildlife in the garden makes it a more rewarding place and reduces the need for chemical control of pests. Many wild flowers can be grown in borders where they may compete for beauty with garden varieties.

An interest in permaculture in the last few years is reflected in the revival of the cottage garden style of gardening. Every available niche is used to grow perennial plants. For example, a clematis will quite happily twine through a wall-rose or over a border shrub. This form of growing is ideal for a small garden where a much greater number and variety of plants can be grown. This ebullient profuse style copies nature so is not recommended for the tidy-minded gardener! Nature is often beautiful but rarely tidy. Colour, scent, texture together with serenity, birdsong and beauty will be yours in a cottage garden.

1. Framing and Forming

All gardens need their lines and boundaries drawn and this is true of even the abundantly planted cottage garden.

WALLS

THE SPECIALIZED HABITAT OF THE WALL has long been used by the cottager where ground space was limited. The sharp drainage of walls makes them ideal for alpine plants which will seed down readily and require little attention. Damp walls quickly become colonized by native ferns. Tall brick walls can be wired with vine eyes and planted with climbers or espalier fruit trees.

Grow scented shrubs to hang over walls, such as **roses** and **philadelphus** (mock orange). A good plant for the top of walls, shown below, is *Saxifraga* **'Aureopunctata'** (variegated London pride) with its leafy, mat-forming rosettes and pink flowers on thin stems. To its left is a **helianthemum** (rock rose), a spreading small shrub that flowers profusely in midsummer. In damper parts of walls, **ferns** will thrive, whilst plants such as the yellow *Corydalis lutea* (on the left) and purple **aubrieta** will seed into crevices.

STEPPING OUT

THE OLD CINDER PATHS AND STEPS of cottage gardens were purely functional, taking the shortest route to privvy or pigsty. When laying a path, playing around with curves which lead to focal points such as seats can make paths an interesting framework for the small garden.

***Saxifraga moschata* (Mossy saxifrage)** A cushion plant, spreading over rocks and soil, which carries slender stems with terminal flowers in shades of red, pink or white. ◑, E, 20 × 45cm/ 8in × 1½ft

When making steps ensure the uprights are securely retained by stones or treated timber.

Place aromatic plants near a path to enjoy the fragrance which is released by touch. Herbs are excellent 'path-edgers'.

Old-fashioned pinks (dianthus) love to spread over dry surfaces without increasing from their root base. Trim after flowering.

Campanula poscharskyana
Profusely-flowering plant, forming a low spreading clump. Early summer.
25 × 60cm/10in × 2ft

Erigeron karvinskianus
Delicate daisy flowers are produced throughout the summer. Not fully hardy. ○, 15cm/6in × wide spread

◆ *This plant loves to freely seed on stone steps and in path crevices.*

The outline of this straight path is broken by attractive clumps of **Santolina neapolitana**. Santolinas, which are lovers of free-draining warm soils, produce masses of button flowers in summer. ○, E, 60 × 60cm/2 × 2ft

◆ *Santolinas are aromatic shrubs, hardy except in severe winters. Prune hard in late spring.*

MIXING MATERIALS IN PATHWAYS can be very effective; stone, gravel and slabs in matching tones when placed carefully provide a valuable foil for plants in adjoining borders. If in doubt keep to one material but this need not be a dull solution as brick and stone can be charmingly set.

Thymes spread easily between stones of paths, withstanding some treading. Aromatic and colourful. ○, E, 10 × 60cm/4in × 2ft

Lysimachia nummularia **(Creeping Jenny)** Groundcover edging plant preferring moist soils. 15cm/6in × wide spread.

The outline of this path is made more interesting by planting of both tall and medium-height plants next to the path.

◆ *Dead-head plants next to gravel paths to avoid seeding.*

HEDGES

CLIPPED HEDGES AND TOPIARY have long been a feature of old cottage gardens. Almost any hedging shrub can be used for topiary. Picket fences and woven hazel hurdles provide attractive barriers and backdrops to newly planted hedges or borders. Hazel hurdles have been used for hundreds of years to separate areas of the garden and to protect from stock and wind.

A natural hedge of native trees and shrubs, clipped occasionally, provides a valuable habitat for wildlife.

***Viburnum opulus* (Guelder rose)** Large spreading shrub ideal for planting in a mixed hedge with wonderful autumn tints and red berries (poisonous). White flowers in umbels in late spring. 4m/13ft

Some hedges, such as *Lonicera nitida* and box may have to be wired when a straight edge is needed.

When planting a double hedge, stagger the two lines of planting to thicken the base.

***Taxus baccata* (Yew)** Traditionally used for clipping and topiary. All parts are poisonous. E, 12m/40ft

***Crataegus* (Hawthorn)** Small tree or can be clipped in a more formal hedge. White, pink or red flowers in early summer. 9m/30ft

***Ligustrum ovalifolium* 'Aureum'** Golden form of privet. Needs clipping two or three times a year. E or semi-E. 2.7m/9ft

***Buxus sempervirens* (Box)** Aromatic, glossy leaves. Slow-growing, ideal for a low hedge. E, 3m/10ft

***Rosa* 'Roseraie de l'Haÿ'** Vigorous shrub rose. Large attractive hips. Early summer to autumn. 2 × 2m/6 × 6ft

ON A DIFFERENT LEVEL, there are the low-growing relaxed plants that lend themselves to use at the front of beds or beside paths. Often sprawling but rarely unwelcome, they can be allowed to tumble at the feet of larger plants behind them. Some, like the pinks, can be also used to make an informal ribbon at the edge of small borders.

Dianthus **'Mrs Sinkins'** Double, deliciously clove-scented flowers. Also pink form. Summer. ○, E, 20 × 30cm/8in × 1ft

Geranium sanguineum **(Bloody cranesbill)** Flowers in early summer. Dead-head for repeat flowering. 25 × 30cm/10in × 1ft

Phuopsis stylosa Spreads into large clumps. Pale pink flowers in summer. Tolerates moist soil. 12.5 × 60cm/5in × 2ft

Stachys byzantina **(Lamb's ears)** Downy leaves with flowering spikes of pink/purple. Spreads to large clump. ○, 45 × 60cm/1½ × 2ft

Viola cornuta alba Spreads to dense tuft by rootstock. Flowers white, pale blue or mauve throughout summer. 7.5 × 60cm/3in × 2ft

Alchemilla mollis **(Lady's mantle)** Downy, rounded leaves. 45 × 60cm/1½ × 2ft

◆ *Gather flowering spikes when fully opened to dry for winter decoration.*

QUIET TIMES

Lonicera periclymenum **'Graham Thomas'** Grow this honeysuckle into trees or on pergolas and walls. 6m/20ft

Laburnum × watereri **'Vossii'** Small tree with many long racemes of yellow flowers in early summer. All parts are poisonous. 6m/20ft

Rosa **'Zéphirine Drouhin'** Shrub rose which can be trained as a climber up to 4m/13ft. Early to late summer.

Clematis viticella **'Etoile Violette'** Vigorous climber with deep purple flowers 10cm/4in. in diameter throughout summer. Prune dead wood in spring. 6m/20ft

Position garden seats to provide pleasing views of the garden or vistas beyond.

Garden paths leading to seats and arbours are a timeless feature of old gardens and they should be positioned with care.

The best seats are simple ones. Anything grand, elaborate or too modern looks out of place.

Rambling roses with plenty of growth around their base often provide better subjects for arches than climbing roses which may be bare and straggly and are better suited to walls. Here the same variety rose has been planted on each side of a simple rustic arch.

◆ *Once-flowering roses may have clematis growing up with them to provide interest later in the summer.*

SEATS, TRELLISES, ARBOURS AND BOWERS were all features of cottage gardens, especially the grander romantic garden of the eighteenth and nineteenth century. Trellises are ideal for providing shelter, screens and vertical dimensions in flat gardens. Trellises and arches should harmonize in style and materials and provide support for a variety of plants grown in sun and shade. Climbers with pendant flowers are well-suited to bowers as it is possible to see into their blossom.

Lilium regale One of the most beautifully scented white lilies. Well-suited to growing in pots and placed by a seat. 1m/3ft

A variety of climbing plants can be grown together. Careful pruning can prevent one plant dominating the growing space.

Scent overhead from climbers on a bower as well as to hand from potted plants is worth planning.

Aromatic plants such as rosemary (*Rosmarinus officinalis*), lavender (*Lavandula*) and southernwood (*Artemisia abrotanum*) provide fragrance next to garden seats. Treneague chamomile planted in crevices underfoot adds pineapple scent.

◆ *Crevice plants often need ample moisture in the soil to thrive and spread over stones.*

2. ROSES AND CLIMBERS

A cottage garden could never be without roses and the climbing plants that adorn its walls and trees.

With their range of habits, foliage and flowers, old shrub roses are perfect for the informal style of cottage gardening. At the back of this picture the tall, arching species rose, ***Rosa glauca*** (syn. *R. rubrifolia*), grows up to 4m/13ft. In front of it is ***Rosa* 'Sarah van Fleet'** a dense, thorny, scented shrub flowering recurrently all summer. ***Rosa* 'Fantin-Latour'** (in the foreground) grows as a large, spreading shrub (2m/6ft) with scented flowers in clusters, blooming in midsummer.

OLD VARIETIES OF ROSES survived in cottage gardens when the grand houses were landscaping with exotic trees and shrubs and creating large parks. Although rarely repeat-flowering, their scented flowers and leaves and soft hues will be reward enough for their space in the mixed border. Pruning can take the form of a light trim after flowering or a more severe clip in spring to improve their shape when their growth becomes lax. Other plants such as sweet peas can be grown through them to provide interest later in the summer.

Hardy geraniums such as pink *Geranium endressii* and blue *G. himalayense* are ideal ground-cover beneath roses.

OLD SHRUB ROSES

Rosa 'Charles de Mills' A gallica rose growing to an erect bush. Beautifully scented, flat and quartered flowers. Its petals can be dried to make pot pourri. ○, 1.5 × 1.5m/5 × 5ft

Rosa 'Complicata' A hybrid between *Rosa gallica* and *Rosa canina* (Dog rose), it develops into a large shrub which can climb into a tree. It has large single flowers up to 12.5cm/5in in diameter. ○, ultimately to 3 × 3m/10 × 10ft

SHADE CLIMBERS

IN COTTAGE GARDENS WHERE SPACE WAS LIMITED, no habitat was left without plants. An old tree or shaded wall can be brightened by a shade-tolerant climber. Dark foliaged climbers can create an interesting 'gloomy' corner, or golden plants can provide light. The latter do particularly well in shade as they often scorch in sun, which is equally true of variegated plants. Finally, there are a few valuable roses which tolerate a degree of shade and still give a prolific display of blossom.

Rosa 'Félicité et Perpétue' Clusters of small, double, blush, fragrant flowers in summer. 7m/23ft

◆ *Position by a sheltered wall for most profuse flowering.*

Rosa 'New Dawn' Repeat-flowering and fragrant. May be grown as a climber or rambler. Subject to mildew if roots are dry. 6m/20ft

Rosa 'Madame Plantier' Alba rose often grown as a climber. Strong-growing with lush green leaves. 2m/6ft

Lonicera tragophylla Best grown into a tree. Beautiful, but not scented, flowers in midsummer in terminal clusters. 9m/30ft

SHADE CLIMBERS

Hydrangea anomala ssp. *petiolaris* (**Climbing hydrangea**) Self-clinging and strong-growing with large corymbs of white flowers in summer. Ideal for a shady wall or to climb a tree. 15m/49ft

◆ *Can be grown as a shrub or trained over an old tree stump.*

Hedera helix **'Goldheart'** Leaves with large yellow splash. This ivy is ideally planted on a north wall but will quickly reach the eaves of a house. 9m/30ft

When planted on house walls, ivies need to be pruned down to 60cm/2ft from the roof line each year.

Golden and variegated plants grow best in dappled shade to prevent scorching of leaves in full sun.

Soil can become very dry even in shade, especially under trees, so avoid planting moisture-loving plants here.

Clematis viticella **'Abundance'** Small crimson flowers produced freely in summer and early autumn. Ideal for growing into shrubs and trees. 3m/10ft

◆.*Prune by removing dead wood in spring rather than cutting down indiscriminately.*

SUN LOVERS

WARM SUNNY CORNERS are ideal for many climbing plants, especially those which are a little tender. Trellises can be used to create this habitat in a sheltered part of the garden. Scented climbers release their aroma more readily in full sun. Care must be taken that the roots of plants such as clematis receive enough moisture when planted in full sun. It will save time if any climber which has a large appetite for water is well mulched in spring. This involves covering the earth around its feet.

Rosa **'Albertine'** A rambler and an old favourite despite some tendency to mildew. It produces only one display of flowers (midsummer) but is immensely floriferous during that time. 6m/20ft

Plants such as the passion flower which climb by tendrils are ideal for growing through roses on walls.

Clematis montana can quickly reach the roof of a house and clog drain pipes and lift roof tiles!

Plants which climb by twining around supports may 'strangle' plants they are growing with.

Rosa **'Rambling Rector'** Rampant hybrid rose forming a dense clump or growing up through a large tree. Small semi-double white flowers in corymbs with yellow anthers. Midsummer. 12m/40ft

Rosa **'American Pillar'** Small-flowered rambler with scentless deep pink flowers with white centre. Good for arches and pergolas. Midsummer. 5.5m/18ft

Clematis montana Rampant climber, flowering profusely in early summer. Flowers best in full sun. 6m/20ft+

Vitis vinifera **'Purpurea'** Black fruits and ornamental foliage. An attractive vine when trained in silver foliaged trees. 6m/20ft

Jasminum officinale (**Summer jasmine**) Semi-evergreen foliage and very fragrant white flowers. 4.5m/15ft

Solanum crispum **'Glasnevin'** Needs to be in sheltered position. Flowers are very fragrant. Summer/autumn. 6m/20ft

Wisteria sinensis Fragrant flowers in slender racemes up to 25cm/8in long. Early summer. 12m/40ft

Rosa **'Paul's Himalayan Musk'** Rampant climber with sweetly scented flowers in hanging corymbs. Midsummer. 12m/40ft

Parthenocissus quinquefolia (**Virginia creeper**) Rampant climber. Leaves are red in autumn but soon fall. 12m/39ft

SUN LOVERS

Passiflora caerulea (**Passion flower**) Strong climber needing a sheltered position. Flowers borne singly on large stalks. Climbs by tendrils. 4.5m/15ft

Some climbers such as wisteria can be grown as standards by initial support of the central trunk.

Spend time concreting trellis and arches firmly in the ground. There's nothing sadder than a collapsed rose arch!

When planting rambler roses, clear a large area of turf around to ease the task of weeding at the base.

SUMMER ONLY

Ipomoea (**Morning glory**)
Heart-shaped leaves and twining stems with single open flowers in shades of blue, pink and lilac. Open in morning sun. Mid to late summer. ○, 2m × 30cm/ 6 × 1ft

Wild vetches and vetchlings are attractive when allowed to grow up through other plants such as early-flowering shrubs.

Perennial sweet pea species such as *Lathyrus latifolius* can scramble over hedges and buildings but have no fragrance.

The old wood of ornamental brambles and raspberries dies back each year and flowers are formed on the new growth of the previous year, so prune with care in autumn.

SOME HERBACEOUS PLANTS exploit the hedgerow habitat to reach sunlight, including many members of the pea family. Herbaceous climbers can also be grown up established wall climbers, such as roses and honeysuckle, and sprawl over trees and shrubs in the border. Old-fashioned varieties of sweet peas grow well through shrub roses, their flowers always finding the sun.

Even some climbing vegetables, whether edible like runner beans or decorative like gourds, can be exploited attractively for their habits.

Tropaeolum majus
(**Nasturtium**) Flowers throughout summer. Well-suited to pot growth. ○, 2.4m × 45cm/8 × 1½ft

Tropaeolum speciosum Deep red flowers on climbing herbaceous stems. Ideal in evergreen hedge. Summer. 4.5m/15ft

Climbing vegetables such as runner beans and climbing French beans grow well over arches covered with plastic mesh or netting. The beans are easily picked and make an attractive feature in a small garden. Sweet peas may be grown amongst them.

◆ *Simple plastic-coated arches are best for climbing vegetables and make for easy maintenance in winter.*

Lathyrus odoratus (**Sweet pea**) Scented flowers, pink, white, purple and lilac shades throughout summer in loose sprays. There are many named varieties and cultivars. Traditionally grown on hazel boughs lining the path to the cottage door, their sweet fragrance fills the air all around. Popular cut flower. The seeds of this hardy annual may be set in early spring but the plants are cut down by severe frosts. ○, 3m/10ft

Lathyrus odoratus **'Painted Lady'** This small-flowered deliciously scented variety has been in cultivation for centuries. Flowers two shades of pink.

3. COTTAGE GARDEN MAINSTAYS

There are plants which are so characteristic that one cannot imagine a cottage garden without them.

TALLER COTTAGE PLANTS

NOTHING EPITOMIZES A COTTAGE GARDEN MORE than the wealth of tall herbaceous plants that have been cultivated in them for hundreds of years. They were often grown so close together that no staking was necessary. Where land for growing food was scarce, the flower garden was often limited to a small strip next to the cottage or by the garden gate. Plants were swopped by neighbours and roots brought back by workers from the 'big house'. Wild flowers were introduced, especially those with double flowers or variegated leaves.

Dictamnus albus purpureus **(Burning bush)** This plant forms dense clumps with pink or white flowers in summer on long spikes. Aromatic leaves. 75 × 75cm/ 2½ × 2½ft

◆ *It prefers well-drained soil and light shade. On hot days, the oils produced by the leaves can be set alight.*

***Geranium pratense* 'Mrs Kendall Clark'** This form of meadow cranesbill grows into a large clump. Early summer. 1 × 1m/3 × 3ft

◆ *This will naturalize in open grassy places.*

***Campanula persicifolia* 'Telham Beauty'** An excellent border plant for sun or semi-shade. Summer. 1m × 45cm/3 × 1½ft

Lysimachia clethroides
forms a large clump in
moist soil, producing white
flowers in terminal curving
spikes. It is ideal for the
woodland border. Summer.
1 × 1m/3 × 3ft

Tall plants that rarely need staking
are valuable plants in the massed
planting of a border. Such a plant
is the pale yellow ***Cephalaria
gigantea*** growing up to 2m/6ft,
forming large clumps. Its flowers
are a valuable source of nectar. In
the foreground, ***Campanula
latiloba*** grows to 1m/3ft in sun or
semi-shade, forming dense mats.
Framing borders by clipped
hedges of box (*Buxus*) or *Lonicera
nitida* helps support taller plants.

Taller Cottage Plants

Phlox 'White Admiral' One of the many scented forms of *P. paniculata*. Prefers slightly moist soil. Summer. 75 × 60cm/2½ × 2ft

Midsummer in a cottage garden is a time of maximum growth. Plants associated with summer abundance begin to flower now, many providing valuable nectar for bees which ensure fertilisation in the kitchen garden. A mix of taller plants among lower growing flowers in cottage beds will emphasise the feeling of profusion.

Euphorbia amygdaloides var. ***robbiae*** Creeping underground rhizomes form dense patches. Best naturalized beneath shrubs. ◐, ●, E, 60 × 60cm/ 2 × 2ft +

Cutting back geraniums and campanulas after flowering may induce second flowering in late summer.

Plants with grey, downy foliage may be prone to mildew in damp conditions. Most thrive in warm, well-drained sites.

Lilies grown in pots and kept free of slugs can be used to fill gaps in borders after early summer flowering. Choose later-flowering, fragrant varieties.

Lychnis coronaria atrosanguinea A short-lived perennial preferring dry soils in full sun. Freely self-seeds. 60 × 45cm/2 × 1½ft

***Papaver orientale* 'Charming' (Oriental poppy)** Large crushed tissue flowers borne singly. 1 × 1m/3 × 3ft

***Asphodeline lutea* (Yellow asphodel)** Spikes densely covered with star-like flowers. Midsummer. 1m × 60cm/3 × 2ft

***Geranium sylvaticum* 'Mayflower'** This cultivar produces a mass of blue-purple flowers in late spring. 1m × 60cm/3 × 2ft

***Alcea rosea* (Hollyhock)** Shades from dark maroon to pink and pale yellows. Late summer. 2m × 60cm/6 × 2ft

Anemone × hybrida **(Japanese anemone)** White, pink or rose flowers. Late summer/autumn. 1.2m × 60cm/4 × 2ft

Geranium psilostemon Large, free-flowering plant making excellent ground cover amongst shrub roses. Mid to late summer. 1 × 1m/3 × 3ft

Acanthus spinosus **(Bear's breeches)** Leaves deeply cut and spiny. Large spikes of flowers in mid to late summer. 1.2 × 1m/4 × 3ft

Lilium candidum **(Madonna lily)** Grows best in well-drained chalky soil, rich in humus. Midsummer. 1.2m × 30cm/4 × 1ft

Polemonium caeruleum album Self-seeding perennial. Flowers produced in early summer. 1.2m × 30cm/4 × 1ft

Polemonium reptans **'Lambrook Mauve'** Pale lilac-blue flowers in loose clusters. Early summer. 60 × 60cm/2 × 2ft

Iris germanica **(Bearded iris)** Various colours and forms. Early summer. ○, 1m × 60cm/3 × 2ft

◆ *Bearded irises and Oriental poppies complement each other perfectly.*

THE NATURAL STYLE OF COTTAGE GARDENS enables plants to die down in autumn without being cut back. Attractive seed heads provide form in the garden during the winter months.

Campanula persicifolia
Drooping open bells. Blue, white and double forms including 'cup and saucer'.
75cm × 45cm/2½ × 1½ft

Campanula alliariifolia
Flower bells hang to one side of a tall stem in summer. Moist soil. ◑,
75cm × 45cm/2½ × 1½ft

***Nepeta × faassenii* (Cat-mint)** Sprays of lilac-blue flowers in midsummer. Aromatic foliage.
45 × 45cm/1½ × 1½ft

***Aconitum napellus* (Monkshood)** All parts are poisonous. Late summer.
1.2m × 45cm/4 × 1½ft

Delphiniums Flowers from cream to blue and deep purple. Summer.
1.5m × 60cm/5 × 2ft

◆ *Cover crowns with grit in spring against slug attack.*

Achillea filipendula **'Gold Plate'** Achilleas attract beneficial insects to the garden. Mid/late summer. ○, 1.2m × 60cm/4 × 2ft

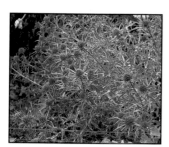

Eryngium bourgatii Thistle-like heads in mid/late summer over deeply cut leaves. ○, 60 × 30cm/2 × 1ft

Campanula latiloba alba Spreads to large clump with pyramidal spikes and masses of open flowers. 60 × 60cm/2 × 2ft

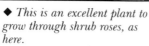
◆ *This is an excellent plant to grow through shrub roses, as here.*

Paeonia lactiflora **'Bowl of Beauty'** Scented flowers in which stamens are replaced by petal-like filaments. Grows to a large clump. Summer. 1 × 1m/3 × 3ft

Aster novi-belgii **'Fellowship'** Spreads to large clump and rarely needs staking. Needs thinning by division every few years to prevent it getting 'woody'. Nectar plant. Late summer. ○, 1 × 1m/3 × 3ft

Penstemon **'Red Knight'** Penstemons are wonderful long-flowering plants. Mid to late summer. E, 1m × 45cm/3 × 1½ft

Kniphofia **'Atlanta'** Forms large clumps with red and cream inflorescence. Early summer. ○, E, 1m × 45cm/3 × 1½ft

Physalis alkekengi **(Chinese lantern)** Long cultivated for bright orange seed heads dried for winter decoration. 45 × 60cm/1½ × 2ft

111

SHADY PLACES

Anemone blanda Spring flowers up to 3cm/1½in. in diameter. Blue, mauve, pink and white forms. Naturalizes in grass beneath trees. 15 × 10cm/6 × 4in

Lysimachia punctata (Garden loosestrife) Large, spreading perennial. Will naturalize in moist places. Summer. 75 × 60cm/ 2½ × 2ft

Primula sieboldii alba Flowering stems with up to twenty flowers; frilled edges. Also pinkish-purple forms. 20 × 30cm/8in × 1ft

◆ *This is not the hardiest of primulas but thrives in a sheltered damp place.*

Symphytum 'Hidcote Blue' Excellent for naturalizing in damp woodlands or ditches. Flowers in spring. 60 × 60cm/23 × 2ft

Lamium maculatum roseum This deadnettle makes excellent ground cover. Pale pink flowers in spring. 30 × 60cm/1 × 2ft

Allium moly Summer flowers in terminal umbels. Naturalizes in well-drained semi-shade. 23 × 30cm/ 9in × 1ft

Primula elatior (Oxlip) Hybrid between *P. veris* (Cowslip) and *P. vulgaris* (Primrose), which naturalizes in shade. Late spring. 30 × 30cm/1 × 1ft

Geranium clarkei 'Kashmir White' Ideal for underplanting roses and light-shade shrubs. Summer. 45 × 45cm/ 1½ × 1½ft

DAPPLED SHADE will support a rich variety of herbaceous plants, many providing ground cover. A garden seat under an old tree is an ideal way to enjoy the garden on a hot summer's day. Golden and variegated plants prefer partial shade to prevent scorching.

Soil in shade may be damp or dry in midsummer. Check before planting up that a site damp in spring retains some moisture in high summer.

Dappled shade will support a wide range of flowers. Delicate, leafy plants will grow in parts of the garden not in direct sunlight.

Golden plants add interesting patches of light in partial shade and their yellow leaves are not scorched by strong sunlight.

Mertensia virginica **(Virginia cowslip)** The plant flowers in spring and is dormant by midsummer. 60 × 45cm/2 × 1½ft

Pulmonaria saccharata **(Lungwort)** Leaves are well-spotted and flowers blue and purple. Spring. 30 × 45cm/1 × 1½ft

Polygonatum × hybridum **(Solomon's seal)** Naturalizes in woods and old garden sites. Early summer. 1m × 30cm/3 × 1ft

Convallaria majalis **(Lily of the valley)** Forms spreading mats by rhizomes in woods and scrub. Several varieties are in cultivation including a pink form.

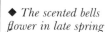
◆ *The scented bells flower in late spring*

GROW WILD

A SMALL MEADOW PATCH enhances any garden. Wild flowers can easily be introduced by putting well-established plants into the ground or by sowing seeds on bare earth. Best results are obtained if the plot is cut once or twice at about the same time each year. The cut herbage is left to dry so that seeds can fall to the ground, and is then removed. A nutrient-poor patch of ground is ideal for a wild flower garden, preventing grasses from dominating. Wild flowers are then able to spread freely.

***Primula vulgaris*
(Primrose)** Shady banks and woods. The pale simple flowers are one of the first signs of spring. 15 × 15cm/ 6 × 6in

Swathes of uncut grass by neat lawns can give a soft and dreamy feel to a cottage garden. Removal of unwanted plants and careful introduction of new ones can create an effect that pleases the eye.

Mown paths, leading to sitting areas in a 'wild meadow', provide viewing spaces to see both plants and the many insects in this habitat.

***Geranium pratense*
(Meadow cranesbill)**
Flowers best in open site or sunny hedge-bank.
Summer. 1m × 60cm/3 × 2ft

***Ornithogalum umbellatum*
(Star of Bethlehem)** Forms a pyramidal raceme. Clump-forming. Spring. 45 × 30cm/1½ × 1ft

***Scilla non-scripta* (Bluebell)**
Fleshy linear leaves with central flower stems. Naturalizes in woods and hedgebanks. Very fragrant. Spring. 45 × 30cm/1½ × 1ft

◆ *Bluebells flower best in dappled sunlight rather than deep shade.*

***Knautia arvensis* (Field scabious)** Growing in meadows and on dry banks, it flowers in midsummer. 45 × 30cm/1½ × 1ft

***Pentaglottis sempervirens*
(Alkanet)** Intense blue flowers mix well with *Silene dioica* (Red campion). Late spring. 70 × 30cm/2¼ × 1ft

Papaver rhoeas (Field poppy) Self-seeding in open ground, gravel and sparse grassland on a variety of soils. Summer. 60cm/2ft

Campanula rotundifolia (Harebell) Hardy plant of sparse grassy places. Mid- to late-summer. 20 × 10cm/ 8 × 4in

Silene dioica (Red campion) Self-seeding perennial. Late spring/early summer. 1m × 30cm/3 × 1ft

When sowing a wild flower garden, sow different species in drifts of differing shapes and sizes. If sowing a mixture of herbs and grasses, sow thinly to avoid grasses dominating other seedlings.

Cardamine pratensis (Lady's smock) Naturalizes in moist grassland. Pale lilac flowers. Also a double form. Spring. 30 × 20cm/1ft × 8in

Filipendula ulmaria (Meadowsweet) Musky scent and 'frothy' cream flowers. Damp soil. Summer. 60cm/2ft

The rich diversity of life sustained by the tall herbage of wild flowers and grasses can be enhanced by the introduction of old garden varieties.

◆ *Clipping back vegetation in late summer allows for vegetative regeneration before winter sets in.*

SELF-SEEDERS

MUCH OF THE APPEAL OF AN INFORMAL BORDER is the chance appearance of self-sown plants. Freshly cultivated old cottage garden soil often throws up a variety of annuals such as poppies. A collection of annual seeds mixed in a bucket with little soil can be sown amongst perennials in a border. This random sowing gives a more natural effect than contrived sowing of single varieties in drifts.

The self-seeding of hardy annuals and biennials such as *Lunaria annua alba* (white honesty), *Meconopsis cambrica* (Welsh poppy) and *Myosotis* (forget-me-not) are reminiscent of the natural distribution of plants in the wild: dense patches, becoming sparser, as one species merges into another in drifts between perennial clumps and shrubs. Contrived sowing results in a tidier garden but may lose much of the charm of the so called 'untidy' garden.

Clarkia elegans White, purple, scarlet and salmon shades. Early summer. ○, 60 × 30cm/2 × 1ft

Iberis umbellata **(Candytuft)** A hardy annual with flowers of purple shades, in early summer. ○, 30 × 20cm/1ft × 8in

Lunaria annua **(Honesty)** A hardy biennial. Large, heart-shaped leaves and scented flowers. Late spring. 1m × 45cm/3 × 1½ft

Lunaria annua alba **(White honesty)**
Seeding in sun or semi-shade, its pure white flowers are lovely in the evening. Late spring. 1m × 45cm/3 × 1½ft

◆ *Flat, paper-like seed pods dry on the stem and can be picked for winter decoration.*

SELF-SEEDERS

IF USING ANNUALS to create drifts of colour, then single varieties can be sown or transplanted in overlapping areas. Careful weeding in spring helps select self-sown annuals as they pop up here and there.

Papaver somniferum (**Peony-flowered poppy**) A variable annual with single or double forms from pale lilac to deep pink petals with frilled edges. Summer. 1m × 30cm/3 × 1ft

Delphinium gracilis (**Rocket larkspur**) Hardy annual with long, loose racemes of blue or violet flowers. Flower spike can be dried. Midsummer. 1m × 30cm/ 3 × 1ft

Salvia sclarea turkestanica A robust form of clary sage. Well-drained, sunny place. Midsummer. 1.2m × 60cm/ 4 × 2ft

Meconopsis cambrica (**Welsh poppy**) Annual or short-lived perennial. Early summer 30 × 30cm/1 × 1ft

Aquilegia vulgaris (**Columbine**) Shades of mauve, purple, pink and white. Early summer. 1m × 45cm/3 × 1½ft

Hesperis matronalis (**Sweet rocket**) Self-seeding, short-lived perennial. Wonderful fragrance. Early summer. 1.2m × 30cm/4 × 1ft

Nigella damascena (**Love-in-a-mist**) Flowers in shades of blue, mauve, pink and white. Summer. 60cm × 23cm/2ft × 9in

Myosotis sylvatica (**Forget-me-not**) Biennial or short-lived perennial. Open ground or woodland. Spring. 30 × 15cm/1ft × 6in

Calendula officinalis
(**Marigold**) Hardy annual.
Orange or yellow. Flowers
from spring to winter.
20cm/8in

Limnanthes douglasii
(**Poached egg plant**)
Annual. Open, sunny site
with cool roots. Summer.
15 × 10cm/6 × 4in

Eschscholzia californica
(**Californian poppy**)
Midsummer. ○,
30 × 15cm/1ft × 6in

◆ *Pick the long seed pods
just before they ripen and
dry in a warm place.*

Oenothera biennis (**Evening
primrose**) Fragrant in the
evening. Self-seeding
biennial. Midsummer.
1.2m × 30cm/4 × 1ft

Digitalis purpurea
(**Foxglove**) Short-lived.
White, pink or purple
forms. Early summer.
1.5m × 30cm/5 × 1ft

Viola tricolor '**Sorbet
Mixed**' Annual or short-
lived perennial. Damp,
shaded sites. Summer.
15 × 15cm/6 × 6in

◆ *This may gradually seed
back to wild species.*

Many annual species do not
like being transplanted.
Broadcast sowing into open
ground or in irregular-
shaped drills achieves the
best planting effects in a
cottage garden.

4. BY THE HOUSE

Even in a small garden you will want herbs and sweet-smelling plants close by the house.

CONTAINERS

Ivy-leaved *Pelargonium* **'Yale'**

ALMOST ANY PLANT can be grown in a container providing it is adequately fed and watered. Containers can be used to give height in borders and to provide interesting textures and focal points in the garden. They can be used to raise some plants, such as nasturtiums, above slug-height and tender plants can be moved out to summer borders. Some plants such as the old double primroses and lilies prefer to be freshly cultivated each year and are ideal pot subjects.

Old wheelbarrows make excellent containers for plants such as nasturtiums, courgettes or even potatoes. More decorative planting with geraniums and trailing pelargoniums helps brighten the summer garden.

◆ *Fill the base of the wheelbarrow with upturned turves to help with moisture retention and feeding.*

This witty little bird has been clipped out of box and sits on his nest against the wall.

Courgette (zucchini) grown in a pot within a decorative chimney pot. It will need to be kept well watered to crop.

Strawberries fruit from this jar, where they have been planted within the pouches.

◆ *Give this kind of jar an open position to enable the fruit to ripen on all sides.*

Sempervivums encrust the layers of this wall pot like jewels. A good choice as they are wonderfully decorative, need heat and tolerate drought. Choose those that form small rosettes for such a planting.

Where soil is poor or space needed for vegetable growing, a collection of tender plants in a variety of terracotta or earthenware pots adds interest and colour.

◆ *Large pot-grown exotics can be sunk in borders to fill in spaces later in the season.*

Container-grown plants will need regular feeding and watering so should not be too far from the house.

Container-growing is a chance to be adventurous and experimental with plantings. Many vegetables can be successfully grown in containers and interplanted with decorative plants.

SCENTED PLANTS

***Rosa* 'Président de Sèze'**
One of the best gallica roses
for the garden, its large,
scented flowers are
produced for a single
period in midsummer. ○,
1.2 × 1.2m/4 × 4ft

Clematis montana
'Tetrarose' Bronze foliage
and lilac-rose flowers on a
lovely climber that grows in
any aspect, through large
trees or over out-houses.
Early summer. 9m/30ft

***Syringa* (Lilac)** Flowers
should be removed as they
die. Lilacs prefer a rich,
lime soil and should be
regularly mulched. Early
summer. ○, 5 × 5m/
16 × 16ft

THE THERAPEUTIC EFFECTS OF SCENT have long been used in
gardens with plants such as lavender and rosemary planted
near back doors and along path edges. Few people can
resist running their hands over southernwood on a hot
summer's day. Night-scented plants such as *Hesperis
matronalis* (sweet rocket) were often planted near the house.
A mixed low hedge of aromatic herbs around the vegetable
plot will help to deter insect pests by masking scent.
Branches of aromatic plants such as southernwood can be
laid in bean and pea trenches to deter rodent pests.

Grow scented shrubs such as **lavenders**, scented **roses**, **southernwood** and **santolina** by a sunny seat. Aromatic plants produce volatile oils through the day, releasing them in sunshine and by touch. Scented flowers such as **pinks** produce their fragrance continuously. Pot-grown plants like *Lilium regale* and the tender *Acidanthera bicolor murielae* can be placed by seats when in flower.

HANDY HERBS

A traditional way of growing **parsley (*Petroselinum crispum*)** in a hanging basket. A large basket lined with moss and about twenty small parsley seedlings, provides fresh parsley for months.

Herbs are rarely showy plants but add soft colours, fragrance and attractive foliage to the flower border.

Resist the temptation to place your culinary herbs too far from the back door. Many herbs respond well to being grown in pots so can always be on hand.

Grow aromatic, heat-loving herbs between paving or gravel. The heat from these surfaces helps release aromatic oils in sunshine.

***Mentha suaveolens* 'Variegata' (Pineapple mint)** A decorative mint, but apple mint (*M. rotundifolia*) is preferable for its sweet spearmint flavour. ◖, 60 × 60cm/2 ×2ft

Bergamot, a rose, oregano and the little blue flowers of the annual self-seeding **borage**, (*Borago officinalis*).

***Lavendula* (Lavender)** Hard prune or clip in late spring. Makes an excellent aromatic hedge. Varying heights. ○, E.

***Thymus vulgaris* (Thyme)** Thymes may be clipped as a low, formal hedge or as an edging plant. ○, E, 30 × 30cm/1 × 1ft

***Rosmarinus officinalis* (Rosemary)** Flowers early summer. Very aromatic. ○, E, 1.2 × 1.2m/4 × 4ft

***Melissa officinalis* 'Variegata' (Lemon balm)** Small, round leaves are lemon-flavoured. 60 × 60cm/2 × 2ft

***Laurus nobilis* (Sweet bay)** withstands regular clipping and forms a good hedge in warmer areas. E, 3m/10ft

HERBS ARE AT THEIR BEST when grown in borders with other plants. Many herbs, such as mints, bergamot, lovage and sweet Cicely, prefer moist soil and do not thrive in the well-drained sunny places recommended for herbs such as sage and thyme.

Here a tiny patch of ground is used for growing a variety of vegetables, fruit and herbs.

◆ *The shaded areas beneath fruit bushes grow parsley and alpine strawberries. Mint grows in the hedge.*

Allium schoenoprasum (Chives) Flowers and leaves used in cooking. Provides an attractive border or path-edge plant. 30cm/1ft

Salvia officinalis **'Purpurascens' (Red sage)** Aromatic leaves with blue flower spikes. Early summer. ○, E, 1 × 1m/3 × 3ft

Bronze fennel (*Foeniculum vulgare* 'Purpureum') with pink roses. Summer. 1.5m × 60cm/5 × 2ft.

◆ *The yellow flowers make good seed heads.*

5. Shrubs and Trees

These make a great impact in a small cottage garden, so must be chosen with care.

SMALL TREES *and* SHRUBS

Acer palmatum 'Dissectum'
Deeply lobed leaves turning yellow and red in autumn. Yellow flowers cluster in spring. Can be used as underplanting in moist, well-drained soil. ◖,
1.2 × 1.5m/4 × 5ft

***Arbutus unedo* (Strawberry tree)** A bushy shrub or a small tree with glossy leaves. Very ornamental in autumn/winter when its white flower bells open at the same time as its 'strawberry' fruits that have matured from last year's flowers. E, 5 × 5m/16 × 16ft

***Acer pseudoplatanus* 'Brilliantissimum'**
Maples are a large genus with a wide range of leaf shapes and colours. They are often grown for their attractive autumn colours. 6 × 7m/20 × 23ft

WHERE SPACE IS LIMITED, careful selection of trees and shrubs is necessary, if only to avoid the 'murderous shrubbery' of Victorian times. If you plant shrubs and small trees in groups or add them to mixed borders, allow them unrestricted growth so that their natural shapes can be seen. Clearing around the base promotes growth but the roots should not be disturbed by digging. Climbing plants such as clematis and honeysuckle can be grown into trees and shrubs. Annual climbers like sweet peas can also be allowed to cling or twine over them, for a natural and profuse effect.

Malus × *purpurea* Upright tree. Leaves flushed with purple. Profusely-flowering in spring with single deep cerise flowers 2.5cm/1ft diameter. Dull purple ovoid fruits. 7.5 × 5.5m/25 × 18ft

Crataegus laevigata **'Paul's Scarlet'** Deep cerise double flowers with musky fragrance in late spring. Slow-growing small tree which tolerates a wide range of soils and conditions. 6 × 5m/20 × 16ft

Robinia pseudoacacia **'Frisia' (False acacia)** Yellow leaflets in spring which turn greenish-yellow in summer, and fragrant cream flowers in pendulous racemes in spring. The bark is deeply furrowed and the twigs are spiny. The tree tolerates atmospheric pollution. 9 × 4m/30 × 13ft

◆ *The delicate foliage of robinias throws only light shade which means the tree can be underplanted.*

131

SMALL TREES *and* SHRUBS

THE LIMITED SPACE of the cottage garden means each plant must be 'good value' and provide a combination of attractive flowers and foliage, fragrance, fruit and good autumn colour. Those shrubs that are in flower for a long season are valuable, and so are those that bloom in winter or early spring.

***Exochorda × macrantha* 'The Bride'** Needs well-drained soil and a warm, sheltered spot. Early summer. 2.4 × 2.4m/8 × 8ft

***Syringa vulgaris* (Lilac)** Lilacs are hardy shrubs or small trees with many species and hybrids, which tolerate most soils especially chalk. Their flowers in late spring have a delicious fragrance. 4 × 4m/13 × 13ft

The flutter and hum of butterflies and bees around the flowers of buddleja varieties in late summer is the reward for tolerating their rather uninspiring presence for the rest of the year!

Flowering shrubs such as deutzia and spiraea benefit from a pruning of their flower shoots when flowering has finished.

***Philadelphus* 'Sybille'** Spreading shrub flowering profusely in open sites. Fragrant flowers. Summer. 1.2 × 1.2m/4 × 4ft

***Lupinus arboreus* (Tree lupin)** Spreading sub-shrub which is cut back by a hard winter. Light soils. Summer. 1 × 1m/3 × 3ft

Potentilla fruticosa Spreading shrubs of various flower colours. Some have glaucous foliage. Summer. 1.2 × 1m/4 × 3ft

Paeonia delavayi* var. *ludlowii Tree peony with single pale yellow flowers. Attractive palmate leaves, unusual seedpods and peeling orange bark. Early summer. Ultimately 2.4 × 2.4m/8 × 8ft

◆ *Tree peonies burst into life in spring, when old dead wood can be pruned out.*

Lavatera olbia 'Rosea' with *Clematis* 'Royal Velours'
Fast-growing sub-shrub with pink 'mallow' flowers mid to late summer. Prune out dead wood in spring.
○, 2 × 2m/6 × 6ft

◆ *The rich tones of some of the darker flowered varieties of clematis need careful placing to be effective.*

Kolkwitzia amabilis (Beauty bush) Spreading shrub with arched branches. Profusely-flowering in full sun. Early summer. 2.4 × 2.4m/8 × 8ft

Deutzia × elegantissima 'Rosealind' Fragrant flowers. For all types of fertile soil. Summer. 1.2 × 1.2m/4 × 4 ft

Buddleja davidii Flowers are produced on new wood so prune hard back in late spring in a small garden. ○, 3 × 3m/10 × 10ft

Cotoneaster frigidus 'Cornubia' Arching branches bearing dense clusters of flowers along the stems followed by scarlet berries. Cotoneasters attract birds and insects into the garden. E, 7 × 7m/23 × 23ft

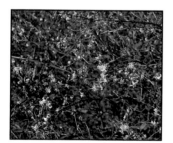

Lonicera fragrantissima Large-spreading shrub. Fragrant flowers in winter. Semi-E in all but coldest climes. 3 × 3m/10 × 10ft

Hamamelis mollis Spreading shrub best grown as standard. Acid, humus-rich soil. Spring. 2.4 × 2.4m/8 × 8ft

Buddleja weyerana 'Golden Glow' Large shrub for a wild corner. Late summer. ○, 3 × 3m/10 × 10ft

SHADY CORNER

MANY FLOWERING SHRUBS AND TREES are shade-tolerant and may be used to provide colour and fragrance in a shady corner. Where mature trees already provide shade, underplant them with golden and variegated-leaved shrubs where they will not be sun-scorched. These can be underplanted with spring-flowering bulbs and shade-tolerant ground cover such as vincas (periwinkles) and hedera (ivies).

Hypericum **'Hidcote'**
Masses of flowers from mid to late summer. Hypericums thrive in a wide range of soils in sun or shade. E or semi-E, 1.5 × 1.5m/5 × 5ft

In a small cottage garden, underplant trees with fragrant, flowering shrubs and put herbaceous ground cover under those shrubs to utilize every niche.

Golden and variegated-leaved shrubs can be planted in shade to give splashes of light and draw the eye towards a focal point such as an arch or seat.

When planting groups of shrubs together, remember that foliage and form are more lasting than blossom or fruit. Plant contrasting textures and shapes.

Cornus kousa Shrub or small tree, not for chalk soils. Summer. 6 × 5m/ 20 × 15ft

Corylopsis sinensis (syn. *C. wilmottiae*) Delicate shrub or small tree with yellow flowers in spring. 4 × 4m/ 13 × 13ft

◆ *The flowers which hang in dense racemes are deliciously scented.*

Philadelphus coronarius **'Aureus'** Hardy shrub with clusters of cream flowers. Golden foliage. 1.5 × 1.2m/ 5 × 4ft

Hardy fuchsias are invaluable for colour in summer/autumn. Delay pruning until spring.

Neillia thibetica Suckering shrub with arching stems. Ideal in mixed border or wild garden. Summer. 2 × 2m/6 × 6ft

◆ *Neillia is especially attractive when grown in a mixed hedge underplanted with geraniums and campanulas.*

The lacecap hydrangeas flowering summer/autumn have particularly graceful flower-heads. This example is 'Blue Wave'.

Clematis armandii A rampant climber when grown in sheltered semi-shade. It has creamy flowers in late spring and glossy leaves. Prune after flowering. E, 6m/20ft+

Camellia japonica **'Nobilissima'** Peony-form flowers in early spring. Camellias need a slightly acid or neutral soil. 3 × 2m/10 × 6ft

◆ *Camellias may need some protection in exposed, cold regions.*

SPACE-SAVING FRUIT

SOME VARIETIES OF SOFT FRUIT, such as raspberries, will tolerate dappled shade. If these fruit bushes are underplanted with alpine strawberries, any awkward shaded corner can become productive. Climbing soft fruit like *Rubus* species (blackberry, bramble, etc.) may also be grown over mature hedges, and pruned down to ground level in the winter.

The warmth and shelter of old walls are ideal for espalier fruit trees such as cherry and pear. Espalier and cordon-grown fruit trees or bushes can be used as living trellises to separate gardens into smaller areas. Rhubarb and marrow will grow on old compost heaps.

Pears generally flower earlier than apples and respond well to being grown in the shelter of an old wall as an espalier. Prune in frost-free winter weather. If planting more than one, allow 6m/20ft between half-standards and 7m/23ft between standards.

Space-Saving Fruit

For many centuries decorative ways of growing fruit trees have been devised. These methods, such as training large shrubs as standards or growing them as cordons and espaliers, are very useful in a small garden where they enable a greater variety of fruit to be included. Here two varieties of apple are growing on low, 'step-over' cordons, and staked, standard gooseberries are underplanted with strawberries.

FRUIT FEASTS

OLD-FASHIONED ORCHARDS with their rich varieties of fruit are becoming a thing of the past. Growing old varieties will help to preserve them and, although cropping may be lighter, the flavour and texture may be superior to modern varieties. Some varieties of apple, such as 'Discovery', crop heavily even on a small tree. Dwarf rootstocks enable most gardens to grow several fruit trees.

Alpine strawberries are accommodating enough to be tucked into odd corners and will tolerate shade.

Spring flowers can be grown under the spreading shade of an apple tree. Plant primulas and narcissi or marrows and rhubarb.

◆ *Remember when planting under fruit trees that you will need to pick the fruit or collect windfalls.*

Blackberry produces a prolific amount of fruit in late summer. Many cultivated varieties. Up to 2m/6ft

Mespilus germanica (**Medlar**) Small, attractive spreading tree. Pear-like fruit. 4 × 4m/13 × 13ft

Currants May be grown as bushes or standards or trained against wall or fence as cordons. Fruit midsummer. 1.2m/4ft

The hardy gooseberry can be grown as a broad bush in a hedge or trained as a small standard. Fruit early summer. 1.2 × 1.2m/4 × 4ft

◆ *The flavour of gooseberries develops well in cool growing conditions. There are dessert or culinary varieties.*

6. WATER

A water feature, no matter how small,
can bring a garden to life.

POOLS WILD *and* FORMAL

***Nymphaea* (Water lily)** An aquatic plant whose floating leaves and flowers provide valuable shade for aquatic life. Stout rhizomes spread quickly in pools and still water.

When starting a new pool allow time for oxygenating plants to become established before introducing larger aquatic plants.

Drainage from pools into marshy areas extends the rich planting sustained by moist habitats. A gravel or stone area around the pool prevents grass species from 'clogging' the pool-edge.

If pools are not fed by natural water, underground pipes can take storm water from the house guttering to the pool.

NO HABITAT IS MORE PLEASING than pools and bogs. Plants quickly become established with lush growth and wildlife such as dragonflies and amphibians soon appear. A garden seat near the pool is a must as is a fence if young children are around. Small formal pools, edged with slabs or stone, with clear water can reflect a shrub or border as well as grow more choice aquatic plants.

Camassia leichtlinii Blue or creamy flowers on long, attractive spikes in late spring. 1m × 30cm/3 × 1ft

***Trollius chinensis* 'Golden Queen'** Plant of moist, shady meadows. There are other paler forms. Early summer. 60 × 30cm/2 × 1ft

***Geum rivale* 'Leonard's Variety'** Water avens tolerate any good garden soil. Early summer. 45 × 45cm/1½ × 1½ft

FORMAL POOL

Planting is restrained to enable shape and reflective qualities of water in the pool to be enhanced. One or two choice species may be added to the water feature.

◆ *Many formal pools have fountains; the therapeutic sound of running water adds to the tranquillity of a garden.*

GRASS EDGES OF WILD POOLS create a cool, humid area around the pond. Informality of outline is helped by planting ornamental grasses, sedges and bamboos, or you may surround it with a bog garden in which you can grow moisture-loving plants you cannot place elsewhere.

Caltha palustris (**Kingcup**) Strong, clump-forming marsh plant. Also white and double forms. 45 × 45cm/1½ × 1½ft

INFORMAL POOL

Planting can include plants such as *Mentha aquatica* (water mint), *Lychnis flos-cuculi* (ragged robin), *Iris pseudacorus* (yellow flag) and aquatic plants such as *Ranunculus lingua* (greater spearwort). Different plants will dominate from year to year.

Plants quickly become established and naturalized in a bog-garden. *Carex pendula* (Drooping sedge) forms a large clump (1.5m/5ft). *Primula japonica* has candelabra whorls of flowers on spikes, (75cm/2½ft) and freely self-seeds. *Iris sibirica* (opposite) grows into a large clump in damp soils in a range of wonderful colours, flowering in early summer. Selective removal of some plants in the bog garden prevents them becoming too dominant.

NEVER DRAIN DAMP AREAS in the garden! They are difficult to create artificially and support a wide variety of attractive plants. These quickly spread or seed down, so weeding is minimal. Stepping stones or raised paths will provide easy access, and underground hoses are useful for very dry seasons. If you do not already have a boggy area, it is worthwhile creating one adjacent to a pond or in a low-lying part of the garden.

Astilbe × *arendsii* **'Erica'** This graceful astilbe forms a large clump in partial shade or sun, but it must have moisture for its roots. It flowers from mid to late summer. 1 × 1m/3 × 3ft

BOGGY BITS

ARTIFICIAL BOGS CAN BE CREATED by hollowing areas to a depth of about 45cm/1½ft and lining them with polythene. Cover the lining with about 15cm/6in of gravel and replace the topsoil in the pit. Try to prevent moisture evaporating by covering the soil with mulch before dry periods occur.

Filipendula rubra large, robust plant with frothy terminal flower heads of deep pink in summer. Forms large clumps in moist soil. 2m/6ft

The foliage of ferns and sedges provides form and interest in boggy areas and helps screen other flowering plants which become dormant in late summer.

Aromatic shrubs such as *Myrica gale* (bog myrtle) will survive in acid boggy conditions and release a wonderful aroma. *Populus balsamifera* (balsam poplar) grows to a large tree with heavy balsam scent.

Willows tolerate moist soils and many varieties have wonderful bark and flower buds for winter and early spring interest.

Thalictrum aquilegiifolium A strong-growing perennial with attractive foliage. Masses of tiny 'frothy' flowers mauve to white. Summer. 1.2m × 60cm/ 4 × 2ft

Primula japonica '**Postford White**' A lovely candelabra primula for semi-shade, flowering in early summer. 45 × 45cm/1½ × 1½ft

146

Athyrium filix-femina (**Lady fern**) Prefers slightly acid soil. Double-pinnate fronds give it graceful form. ◐, 1 × 1m/3 × 3ft

Primula florindae Flowers in a single panicle, yellow or reddish amber-orange. Broad leaves. Summer. ◐, 1m × 60cm/3 × 2ft

Ligularia przewalskii Leaves with irregularly cut margins. Numerous flowers in summer. ◐, 1.5m × 60cm/5 × 2ft

Primula pulverulenta Candelabra whorls of up to twenty flowers in shades of red to white. Summer. To 1 m × 45cm/3 × 1½ft

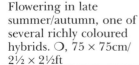

Lobelia '**Dark Crusader**' Flowering in late summer/autumn, one of several richly coloured hybrids. ○, 75 × 75cm/ 2½ × 2½ft

Chaerophyllum hirsutum '**Roseum**' Delicate umbels in late spring, growing from rosette of leaves. 60 × 60cm/2 × 2ft

Leucojum aestivum (**Summer snowflake**) Bell-like flowers. Sun or semi-shade. Summer. 60 × 20cm/ 2ft × 8in

Epilobium angustifolium album (**White rosebay willow herb**) Not as invasive as true form. Summer. 1.2m × 60cm/ 4 × 2ft+

Iris kaempferi (**Japanese flag**) This large-flowered beardless iris is also obtainable in white, pink and mauve forms. Summer. 75 × 75cm/2½ × 2½ft

Beds and Borders

Trees and bulbs will grow happily in grass, but if you want to grow cultivated plants they need to be planted in beds and borders. Here they can be offered the very best conditions in which to grow, free from the competition of weeds. By sympathetically grouping together a diversity of plants a beautiful border can be created.

Ideally the border should be in full or partial sun and sheltered from cold wind. Do not despair if your garden is shaded all day by neighbouring trees or on a windswept hillside. You can have beautiful borders by selecting plants that will thrive in these inhospitable conditions.

The Shape of Your Border

Formal geometric beds in the form of straight-sided rectangles and squares or circles are a good choice for a small garden. The formality can be reinforced by arranging the plants in a repetitive pattern. Alternatively they may be planted in a free informal manner within this formal framework to good effect.

It is more difficult to get a well balanced planting in a bed with natural curves, especially in an island bed. Form has to be created within the planting itself by the use of bold clumps, structural evergreens and architectural plants. Laying a hosepipe on the ground will help you create the shape you want but do not make too many curves. Look at the shape you have created from an upstairs window. Island beds look best in a large garden where there is a view beyond the bed.

If you garden on a hillside you may wish to terrace it with retaining walls to create raised beds.

What to Grow

Annuals, which flower in their first year from seed and then die, are useful for a bed in its first season where perennial weeds are a problem. Thorough digging can be repeated the following winter.

Bedding plants give an instant garden and can be changed with the seasons. This is a good solution for small beds in small gardens but there is no sense of permanence.

Herbaceous borders planted entirely with perennial plants will be very impressive when flowering exuberantly in summer and early autumn but will be of little interest in winter when the plants are resting. They are best suited to large gardens where they can be sited some distance from the house.

Mixed borders using a medley of trees, shrubs, perennials, annuals, biennials and

A harmonious combination of pink dicentra, geranium and thalictrum, mauve nepeta, planted in clumps, drawn together by the ribbon of magenta *Gladiolus byzantinus*.

bulbs can be planned to provide some interest every day of the year. This is the best solution for most gardeners.

The choice of plants is a personal preference but they must suit the soil and climate. Light sandy soils will support a different range of plants to those growing on heavy clay. Soil acidity, measured as the pH, is of importance to some plants: for example rhododendrons and many heathers require an acid soil.

Plants growing well in neighbouring gardens will do equally well for you but you will want to introduce some new ideas. Visit gardens that are open to the public, take a notebook with you and note down plants you like, where they are growing and which plants look good together. Do not be afraid to ask the gardener or the owner about the plants.

Look for plants which have attractive form, good foliage and a long season of interest: plants which produce attractive fruits after flowering or a second crop of flowers.

PREPARING THE SITE

Before any planting can be done the bed needs to be well dug and all perennial weeds removed. If the site is very weedy a herbicide can be used to kill the weeds a few weeks before digging.

On sandy light soils dig in as much compost or manure as you can afford. On heavy clay incorporate grit in addition to these organic bulky manures to improve drainage. If the soil is very badly drained consider making raised beds.

Fish, blood and bone fertilizer applied at planting time will give the plants a good start.

The path leads the way to a seat flanked by twin though different borders of cool colours: mauve nepeta and blue linum.

DESIGNING WITH PLANTS

The aim is to create a harmonious border by marrying good structure with contrasts of colour and texture in flower and foliage.

Flowers are what you first think of, but a border should look good when not in flower. Plants with good form and foliage need to be planned for first.

A sunny border composed of golden kniphofia and coral alstroemeria.

Evergreen shrubs provide a good background to flowers and give solidity to the border. Balance these with flowering shrubs and bold clumps of perennials with architectural merit. Vary the size and shape of these plants contrasting low growing horizontal subjects with rounded forms and the occasional vertical emphasis.

These structural plants are permanent and the space allocated to them needs to accommodate their eventual size. The best way to determine their positions is to plot them on a plan of the border drawn to scale.

Herbaceous plants look best planted in bold clumps and drifts. Although tall plants will generally be planted at the back and short at the front a more interesting picture will be created by bringing the occasional tall plant forward and allowing some short ground-covering plants to flow backwards into the border. Choose flowers of varying form and texture.

As well as grading by size you may wish to grade by colour. Pale colours are easier to blend and harmonize than bright ones. Subtle contrasts of colour and changes of tone can build up to the vivid hues. Flower gardens rarely clash badly but orange-reds need to be kept away from blue-reds. This can be done by separating them with green or silver foliage or pale creamy flowers.

Good foliage is an essential ingredient of a successful border. Green and silver leaves will link the flowering plants and enhance them. Look for contrast in habit, size and texture when choosing foliage. Brightly variegated and red foliage is useful used sparingly.

Good plant associations can lift a border from good to excellent. Try to give every plant the best neighbour you can find for it. Look at associations that please you in other gardens and magazines: you will notice that contrasts of form, texture and colour will have been used. Beware, however, of too much contrast or the planting will appear restless. Calm and stability can be imposed on a border by repeating a good plant at regular intervals to unite the whole.

Allium aflatunense is one of the most ornamental onions, carefully placed against a background of pale pink clematis.

A bed at the foot of a shady wall with ferns, dicentra and pink trillium.

BORDER MAINTENANCE

A newly planted bed will need watering for the first week or so and in dry periods in the first summer.

It is essential to keep on top of the task of weeding because weeds compete with your cultivated plants for water and nutrients as well as looking unsightly.

By removing the dead heads of flowers you will keep the border tidy and encourage the plant to make new flower buds. Do not dead-head plants that are going to produce decorative seed heads or fruits, such as honesty or rugosa roses.

Perennials will in most cases need to be cut to the ground in late autumn. Mulching with compost or manure every year will improve soil structure and fertility. A boost to growth in spring can be given by top-dressing the beds with a general organic or inorganic fertilizer.

Many perennials spread rapidly into big clumps. They need to be lifted, divided and healthy pieces replanted with fresh compost and fertilizer.

Some plants will need staking, but for ease of maintenance choose those that do not. Bamboo canes and string, hazel twigs and

Penstemon is an invaluable plant which flowers over a long period in summer. This rich, dark cultivar is 'Blackbird'.

The glamorous *Tulipa* 'Black Parrot' thrives at the foot of a hot stony wall.

patent metal supports all have a place in staking.

Shrubs, roses and clematis will need pruning, but consult a pruning guide as plants differ as to the time and method of pruning.

If you include annuals and biennials these will need to be raised from seed every year.

THE TIME-SCALE OF A BORDER

A border when planted is not like a finished painting. In time, growth will alter the scale of plants. In a mixed border the structural framework of evergreens and deciduous shrubs will take about five years to reach reasonable maturity. They must be given space at planting time to reach this potential. By all means fill the spaces between them with other plants but in the knowledge that some of these will be overwhelmed by the shrubs as they mature.

The planting is not finite. Plants do not always grow as you expect them to, so be prepared to move them around the border the following season. Our taste changes, as does fashion in plants, so always consider replacing a plant that no longer gives you pleasure.

No border is ever perfect but we can have great fun introducing new ideas in our attempt to make it so.

1. MIXED BORDERS

Borders for all seasons. The choice of plants is personal but suitability of soil and aspect need to be considered.

The COTTAGE GARDEN

IMAGINE A GARDEN OF SWEET DISORDER having no preconceived plan other than a path to the front door edged with lavender and old-fashioned pinks. The entire garden is treated as a mixed border with a miscellany of shrubs, perennials and bulbs interspersed with vegetables and herbs. This timeless haphazard planting translates well to the garden of a small modern house.

A cottage border such as this would undoubtedly be crammed with spring-flowering bulbs such as snowdrops, narcissus, tulips and crocus. The perennials are cut down in the autumn and the annuals pulled up once they have shed their seed.

A fine early summer display of 'Shirley' poppies and stately delphiniums in a cottage garden.

◆ *Both these plants are easily raised from seed.*

A cottage garden border in summer. Sweet peas climbing on a wig-wam of hazel poles are surrounded by an informal planting of typical cottage garden plants: perennial delphiniums and lupins and annual cornflowers and marigolds. The path is edged with pinks, chives and strawberries. Runner beans, attractive in flower and fruit, would be equally suitable for growing on the poles.

COTTAGE GARDEN PLANTS

LUPINS, DELPHINIUMS AND HOLLYHOCKS – such are the cottager's flowers, underplanted with tulips, anemones, primroses and violets. Around them are self-seeding aquilegias, forget-me-nots, foxgloves and easily grown shrubs such as philadelphus or forsythia with gooseberry and blackcurrant bushes. Roses, clematis, honeysuckle and sweet peas complete the picture.

Daphne mezereum
Deliciously scented flowers before the leaves in early spring. There is a white form. 1.2 × 1.2m/4 × 4ft

Lupins look shabby after flowering. Disguise them by siting a taller, later flowering, plant in front.

Allow some aquilegias to self-seed. Interesting forms and colour variations will occur.

Grow parsley and chives as an edging down the side of the garden path.

Digitalis purpurea
Common foxgloves are red, but pink, white, cream and apricot flowers occur. Biennial. 1.2m × 60cm/ 4 × 2ft

Double forms of the primrose are cottage favourites. They are now obtainable in a variety of colours. 15 × 20cm/6 × 8in

Allium schoenoprasum 'Forescate' Pink-flowered form of the common chive. A good edging plant. 30 × 30cm/1 × 1ft

Aquilegia vulgaris 'Nora Barlow' Interesting form of colombine or Granny's bonnet for early summer. 1m × 45cm/3 × 1½ft

Mentha suaveolens 'Variegata' A culinary mint grown for its attractive summer foliage. 30 × 60cm/1 × 2ft

Rosa **'Tuscany Superb'** An old Gallica rose of velvety, dark, blackish crimson, flowering in midsummer. 1 × 1m/3 × 3ft

Paeonia officinalis **'Rubra Plena'** An old cottage garden peony flowering in early summer. Good foliage. 60 × 60cm/2 × 2ft

Alcea rosea Hollyhocks look and grow best in a wall border in full sun. Many colours. 2m × 60cm/6 × 2ft

Lupins are early summer perennials in a wide range of colours and easily seed-raised. ○, 1.2m × 60cm/ 4 × 2ft

Philadelphus coronarius Midsummer flowering shrub. Creamy white flowers. Powerful fragrance. 2.4 × 2m/8 × 6ft

Syringa vulgaris **'Alba'** White form of common lilac, highly scented flowers in early summer. 3 × 2.4m/10 × 8ft

Delphiniums Large-flowered hybrids for early summer. ○, 2.4 × 1m/8 × 3ft

◆ *The stately spikes require discreet staking.*

HERBACEOUS PERENNIALS

THESE PLANTS ARE THE MAINSTAY OF THE MIXED BORDER from spring until autumn. They die to the ground in winter and re-emerge in spring. They establish quickly, flowering well in their first year. Most are easily propagated by division so plant numbers are soon built up.

***Persicaria bistorta* 'Superba'** (syn. *Polygonum*) Self-supporting pink spikes for a long season in summer. ○, 60 × 60cm/ 2 × 2ft

Encourage perennials to flower again by removing dead flower-heads and feeding the plant.

Stake plants early so that by flowering time the stakes will be concealed by foliage.

Many perennials are easily raised from seed sown in early autumn or in the spring.

***Achillea millifolium* 'Lilac Beauty'** Flowers from midsummer until autumn. Attractive feathery foliage. ○, 1m × 60cm/3 × 2ft

Digitalis ferruginea A perennial foxglove with slender architectural spikes of an unusual shade. ●, 1m × 30cm/3 × 1ft

Campanula persicifolia Nodding blue or white bells in summer. Will seed about discreetly. ○, 1m × 30cm/ 3 × 1ft

Penstemon glaber is one of the smaller and hardier penstemons. It will reward you with flowers from early summer until the frosts. Penstemons come in many lovely shades and need a well drained fertile soil in full sun. ○, 60 × 60cm/ 2 × 2ft

◆ *Minimize frost damage by delaying cutting back until late spring. Take easily rooted summer cuttings to replace winter losses.*

A mixed border in early summer. Perennials interlaced with blue forget-me-nots are planted against a back-drop of yellow-leaved shrubs. Deep blue aquilegias and yellow Welsh poppies (*Meconopsis cambrica*) merge prettily together. A white flowered aquilegia with variegated foliage and the bright leaves of *Iris pallida* 'Variegata' make a dramatic splash at the front of the border.

Aquilegia vulgaris The flowers of these long-spurred columbines float like butterflies in early summer. These perennials are very easy to grow from seed. 1m × 45cm/3 × 1½ft

FOLIAGE

AN ABUNDANCE OF HEALTHY GREEN FOLIAGE will enhance the appearance of flowers. Red, silver and variegated leaves are useful but need to be used with discretion. Look for contrast in size, shape and texture of leaf.

Hedera colchica **'Sulphur Heart'** An excellent ivy to grow up a pole or for ground cover. E, climber to 5m/16ft

Stipa tenuissima A soft textured, fine leaved grass which moves gracefully in the breeze. Plumes of feathery flowers are produced in summer. It fades to buff in autumn. ○, 60 × 45cm/ 2 × 1½ft

Symphytum × *uplandicum* **'Variegatum'** Stunning cream variegated foliage for shade. Cut down the lilac spikes after they have flowered. Any plain green leaves that develop should be removed. ●, 1m × 60cm/ 3 × 2ft

Euphorbia nicaeensis The neat silver foliage looks good all the year. Greenish yellow flowers in summer. ○, E, 40 × 60cm/1½ × 2ft

FOLIAGE

Geranium renardii has pretty purple-veined white flowers, but grow it for its lovely textured foliage. ○, 30 × 30cm/1 × 1ft

Alchemilla mollis Downy, soft green, veined leaves. Frothy yellow green flowers. 45 × 45cm/1½ × 1½ft

Alchemilla mollis is a prodigious seeder so remove flowering stems before the seeds ripen.

Many grasses retain their form in winter so delay cutting them down until the spring.

Paulownia is a tree which when young can be cut hard back every spring to produce very large leaves.

Hosta sieboldiana grown principally for its big, textured leaves has cool white flowers. 1 × 1.5m/ 3 × 5ft

◆ *Requires moisture and some shade. Beware of slugs.*

Evergreen Shrubs

EVERGREEN SHRUBS GIVE A PERMANENT STRUCTURE to a border at all seasons and provide an excellent background for flowering plants. Conifers, particularly those of fastigiate or prostrate habit, can be useful but restrict yourself to one or two. Evergreens such as yew, box and holly can be tightly clipped to impose a year-round formality upon the border.

Euonymus fortunei **'Silver Queen'** Creamy white variegation. 1 × 1.5m/3 × 5ft

Brachyglottis **'Sunshine'** (syn. *Senecio*) Silver leaved shrub for a sunny well-drained spot. Yellow flowers. ○, 1.2 × 2m/4 × 6ft

◆ *A blue clematis looks good growing through this shrub.*

Hebe rakaiensis This apple-green rounded shrub is outstanding in the dull days of winter ○, 1 × 1.2m/ 3 × 4ft

Eucalyptus gunnii grown as a shrub by pruning annually in late spring.

The very dark green of **Taxus baccata**, the common yew, gives a permanency to this border and makes an excellent background for the white-flowering shrub and bright perennials.

◆ *The narrowly upright Irish yew,* Taxus baccata *'Fastigiata', is useful for imposing formality on a border.*

Santolina or **'Cotton Lavender'** is an ideal evergreen shrub to clip tightly into balls for formal foliage effect.

Ilex aquifolium **'Ferox Argentea'** A variegated holly, unique in having prickles over the entire leaf surface. No berries. 2.4 × 2.4m/8 × 8ft

A clipped spiral of **Buxus sempervirens**, the common box, planted in a pot adds interest to a border.

FLOWERING SHRUBS

Camellia 'Water Lily'
Flowers in early spring.
Acid or neutral soil and
shade from morning sun
essential. ◑, E, 3 × 2.4m/
10 × 8ft

Space flowering shrubs far
enough apart for them to
achieve their ultimate
spread without
encroachment.

If a spring-flowering
ceanothus needs cutting
back, do this immediately it
has finished flowering.

Buddleja davidii should be
pruned hard in late winter.
Prune *B. crispa* lightly in
late spring.

Ceanothus 'Puget Blue'
Neat-textured evergreen
foliage. Blue flowers in
early summer. ○, E, 1.5 ×
2.4m/5 × 8ft

Buddleja crispa A summer-
long succession of orange-
throated lilac flowers.
Beautiful felted leaves. ○,
2.4 × 2.4m/8 × 8ft

Choisya ternata Glossy
green leaves compliment
the scented white flowers of
Mexican orange blossom.
○, E, 2 × 2m/6 × 6ft

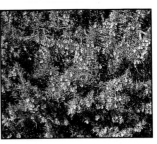

**Rosmarinus officinalis
(Rosemary)** An aromatic
small shrub, flowering in
spring/early summer ○, E,
1 × 1m/3 × 3ft

**Potentilla fruticosa
'Katherine Dykes'** Flowers
late spring until autumn.
Good drainage and full sun.
○, 60cm × 1m/2 × 3ft

**Daphne × burkwoodii
'Somerset'** Variegated,
sweetly scented, white-
throated pink flowers in
spring. ○, 1.5 × 1m/5 × 3ft

**Chaenomeles speciosa
'Nivalis' (Flowering
quince)** Flowers over a long
period in early spring.
1.5 × 1.5m/5 × 5ft

FLAMBOYANT FLOWERING SHRUBS often have a very short flowering period. When choosing them always consider how they will look when not in flower: elegance of habit and attractive foliage are important. Include some with scent to fill your garden with perfume.

Abutilon × suntense Flowers in early summer. Appreciates a warm and sheltered position. ○, 4 × 3m/13 × 10ft

◆ *This is a beautiful shrub but it is not fully hardy.*

Indigofera heterantha Prettily divided leaves. Mauve-pink flowers all summer. ○, 3 × 3m/ 10 × 10ft

Hydrangea villosa The velvety leaves of this shrub set of the lace-cap flowers to perfection. ●, 2.4 × 2m/ 8 × 6ft

Magnolia × loebneri 'Leonard Messel' A narrow elegant tree 4.5 × 2.4m/15 × 8ft

◆ *Winter attraction of branch pattern and buds.*

ROSES

OLD ROSES BLOOM EFFUSIVELY, looking and smelling wonderful in early summer. Look also for roses with a longer or repeated flowering period and those with other attributes such as good foliage, nice hips or interesting thorns. A climbing rose on a wall or up a pole will add another dimension.

If pruned hard *Rosa glauca* will produce no flowers or hips but abundant fresh foliage.

Dead-head roses throughout the season to encourage more flowers – apart from varieties with good hips.

'Cécile Brunner' has perfectly shaped tiny pink buds on a sparse bush. Also available as a climbing rose. 75 × 60cm/2½ × 2ft

'Nevada' A large shrub rose with a spectacular early-summer flowering. A few flowers in autumn. 2.4 × 2.4m/8 × 8ft

'Stanwell Perpetual' is seldom without a sweetly scented flower from early summer until late autumn. 1.5 × 1.5m/5 × 5ft

'Iceberg' The climbing form of this popular cluster rose makes an excellent pillar rose climbing to 2.4m/8ft.

An association of roses with a complementary planting of perennials. **Rosa glauca**, a vigorous shrub with handsome purple-grey foliage, has small single cerise flowers (not shown) followed by red autumnal hips. The double pink, fragrant flowers of **'Mary Rose'** are produced throughout the rose season on a sturdy bush. **Geranium endressii** and **Viola cornuta** complete the picture.

FLOWERS *to plant with* ROSES

FLOWERS IN SHADES OF PINK, PURPLE, LILAC, WHITE AND CREAMY YELLOW associate well with the pinks, whites and crimsons of the old roses. Campanulas, violas and hardy geraniums are excellent companion plants. The brighter tones of modern roses are best complemented by using flowers of similar but softer hues, toned down with cool silver and green foliage.

Clematis viticella **'Purpurea Plena Elegans'** A late-flowering clematis, lovely growing through a pink rose. Climber to 2.4m/8ft

If *Viola cornuta* gets straggly in mid-season, revive it by cutting it right down.

When *Rosa complicata* has finished flowering, prune out all stems that have flowered.

Prune viticella varieties of clematis almost to the ground in late autumn or early spring.

A harmonious mixed border of roses and other plants. *Rosa complicata*, which has large bright-pink single flowers with white and yellow centres, is here associated with white foxgloves and the blue form of *Campanula persicifolia*, the peach-leaved bell flower.

Viola cornuta An easy viola flowering prodigiously. White, lilac and deep violet forms available. E, 30 × 60cm/1 × 2ft

Allium aflatunense A stately ornamental onion to associate with the Burnet roses of early summer. 1.2m × 30cm/4 × 1ft

***Geranium* 'Johnson's Blue'** Intense lavender-blue flowers are lovely planted with pale yellow roses. 30 × 60cm/1 × 2ft

***Artemisia absinthium* 'Lambrook Silver'** Grown for its silky, silver foliage. Highly aromatic. ○, E, 60 × 60cm/2 × 2ft

Nepeta racemosa An excellent edging plant for rose beds. Catmint flowers throughout the season. ○, 45 × 45cm/1½ × 1½ft

***Salvia officinalis* 'Purpurascens'** The purple-leaved form of the shrubby culinary sage. ○, E, 60cm × 1m/2 × 3ft

Stachys byzantina (syn. *S. lanata*, Lamb's ears) forms a carpet of weed-suppressing, woolly, silver leaves. ○, E, 45 × 30cm/1½ × 1ft

Sisyrinchium striatum Iris-like foliage and spikes of creamy yellow flowers which close in late afternoon. E, 60 × 30cm/2 × 1ft

***Geranium* × *riversleaianum* 'Mavis Simpson'** A hybrid geranium which flowers profusely all summer long. ○, 30cm × 1m/1 × 3ft

Geranium sanguineum* var. *striatum A lovely pink form of the bloody cranesbill, flowering for many weeks. ○, 30 × 45cm/1 × 1½ft

◆ *More flowers are induced by cutting back mid-season.*

VERY SMALL BEDS

IT IS OFTEN BEST to treat a very small bed in a formal manner and confine the planting to neat low growing plants with attractive foliage: an edging of box always looks good. Seasonal interest can be introduced with bulbs and bedding plants. In this way changes can be made each year.

Two small square beds are edged with box which is clipped into balls at each corner. A standard 'lollipop' *Euonymus fortunei* 'Emerald 'n' Gold' is planted in the centre. These evergreen shrubs are attractive the year round. This basic planting is enlivened by using seasonal bedding. Seen here with **tulip 'West Point'** and **forget-me-nots**, it could have red pelargoniums in summer.

This bed is also box-edged but here the box is clipped tightly into balls to frame a specimen plant of **Yucca gloriosa** **'Variegata'**.

◆ *Box is easily grown from cuttings so it need not be expensive if you are patient.*

By treating two or more beds identically a sense of unity and permanence is bestowed upon the garden.

Bold plants such as the echeverias, seen here bedded with airy nemesia, make an impact.

◆ *Echeverias are not hardy and need winter protection.*

A WINTER BORDER

A VERY SATISFYING BORDER can be made with winter-flowering shrubs, trees with interesting bark, evergreens, early-flowering perennials and bulbs. Ideally the border should be visible from the house with the low winter sun illuminating it. Alternatively site it by a path or entrance-drive where you walk, as many winter flowers are highly scented.

Jasminum nudiflorum The cheerful winter jasmine has yellow flowers on green stems. It flowers best grown on a wall for support and protection. Climbing to 2m/6ft.

Acer griseum (**Paper-bark maple**) Small tree with cinnamon-brown peeling bark. Glows in winter sunshine. 8 × 6m/26 × 20ft

Salix alba vitellina '**Britzensis**' A willow with glowing orange-red bark on coppiced stems. 1.5 × 1.5m/5 × 5ft

Viburnum × bodnantense '**Dawn**' Pink, scented flowers adorn the naked branches for many weeks. 3 × 2m/10 × 6ft

Hamamelis × intermedia A witch-hazel with fragrant yellow spidery flowers on bare branches. Acid soil, 2.4 × 3m/8 × 10ft

Viburnum tinus A handsome evergreen. White flowers from pink buds in late winter. E, 2.4 × 2.4m/8 × 8ft

Iris unguicularis The Algerian iris has scented flowers throughout the winter. Needs hot dry spot. ◑, E, 60 × 30cm/2 × 1ft

Cyclamen coum Brave little pink or white flowers for many weeks which defy the frost. 10 × 15cm/4 × 6in

Galanthus nivalis Aptly named the harbingers of spring, snowdrops are easy to grow, appreciating some shade. 15 × 15cm/6 × 6in

***Helleborus foetidus* 'Wester Flisk'** Bunches of maroon edged, green flowers over evergreen foliage. E, 45 × 45cm/1½ × 1½ft

Bergenia purpurascens Bold, shiny, green leaves change to burnished red in cold weather. E, 30 × 45cm/ 1 × 1½ft

Heathers and conifers make excellent bed-fellows. Conifers grown for their varying forms and colour changes are enlivened by the heathers in late winter.

◆ *Red, pink or white, winter-flowering heather,* Erica carnea, *will tolerate alkaline soil.*

175

2. Sunny Beds and Borders

Memories of high summer – hot baked earth with silver-foliaged, aromatic plants revelling in these hard conditions.

HOT, DRY BORDERS

ON A SANDY OR STONY SOIL, rain drains through very quickly taking nutrients with it. If the garden is on a slope facing the sun it will be very dry indeed. However, this is exactly what some plants demand: many silver-leaved plants will only thrive in such conditions.

The plants in this very hot, dry, sunny spot have been well-chosen and are obviously thriving. *Cistus* 'Peggy Sammons', penstemon and a graceful dierama are enhanced by silver-leaved shrubs.

◆ *The pots contain purple sage, lavender and a tender aeonium.*

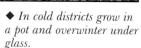

Cistus purpureus An aromatic evergreen shrub which covers itself with bloom in early summer. ◯, E, 1.2 × 1m/4 × 3ft

Convolvulus sabatius displays a succession of lavender-blue flowers on trailing stems all summer long. This convolvulus is not invasive. ◯, 15 × 45cm/6in × 1½ft

◆ *In cold districts grow in a pot and overwinter under glass.*

Helianthemum 'Annabel' A lovely double form of rock rose with a long flowering season. ◯, E, 30 × 45cm/ 1 × 1½ft

◆ *Cut back hard when flowering has finished.*

Yucca gloriosa 'Variegata' An architectural plant with evergreen leaves. E, 1.2 × 1m/4 × 3ft

◆ *Dramatic spikes of white flowers in late summer.*

The seat invites you to bide awhile amongst the fragrant **Madonna lilies (*Lilium candidum*)**. The scented climbing rose **'Golden Showers'** and *Solanum crispum* **'Glasnevin'** flower for many weeks.

THE BORDER AT THE FOOT OF A SUNNY WALL will be very hot on a summer afternoon. Choose plants that enjoy a baking. In winter this will be the warmest spot particularly if the wall is that of a house. Here is an opportunity to try something a little tender that cannot be grown in the open.

Abutilon megapotamicum A graceful wall shrub in flower for the entire summer.
○, 3 × 3m/10 × 10ft

◆ *This is a tender plant but worth trying in a sunny, sheltered corner.*

Agapanthus **Headbourne Hybrids** A very hardy strain of the blue African lily.
○, 60 × 45cm/2 × 1½ft

GRAVEL BORDERS

A GRAVEL BORDER adjacent to a terrace or drive makes an interesting and harmonious link to a lawn. Plants that need good drainage will thrive in this environment. Site in full sun, excavate 15–20cm/6–8in of soil and replace with small limestone chippings.

Dianthus **'Rose de Mai'** An old-fashioned pink of spreading habit with an abundance of flower. ○, E, 20 × 45cm/8in × 1½ft

Erigeron karvinskianus A fascinating little daisy flower. The flowers open white and turn pink with age. ○, 15 × 30cm/6in × 1ft

◆ *This will seed about in a delightful way.*

Erinus alpinus A tiny plant which seeds happily around in gravel. Flowers red, mauve, pink or white ○, E, 7.5 × 7.5cm/3 × 3in

A gravel terrace bed in early summer with pinks, campanulas, diascias and a carpet of pink and white *Thymus serpyllum*. *Erigeron karvinskianus* will be covered with little daisies until the autumn.

◆ *The pot is planted with sempervivums (houseleeks). The evergreen rosettes change colour with the seasons.*

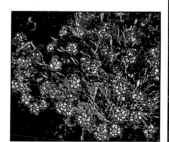

Origanum 'Kent Beauty'
Unusual green and purple papery bracts on trailing stems. Flowers dry well. ○, 15 × 30cm/6in × 1ft

Calamintha nepeta Dainty ice-blue flowers produced usefully in late summer. Aromatic foliage. 45 × 60cm/18 × 24in

Dianthus 'Waithman's Beauty' A distinctly marked, single, old-fashioned pink; it revels in a hot gravelly site. E, 15 × 23cm/6 × 9in

Cut back pinks (dianthus), phlox, aubrieta and alyssum immediately after flowering. New neat foliage grows quickly.

Take cuttings of pinks to replace existing plants as they become leggy and shabby with age.

Do not dead-head pulsatillas or you will miss the lovely seed heads they have.

Phlox subulata 'Betty' A cushion of fine leaves smothered with flowers in early summer. ○, E, 10 × 30cm/4in × 1ft

Armeria maritima (Thrift) From a mat of grass-like leaves arise little stiff-stemmed, round flowers. ○, E, 10 × 20cm/4 × 8in

Campanula poscharskyana A spreading carpeter for gravel but not for small beds. 15cm/6in × indefinite

Diascia 'Ruby Field' One of the hardiest of the diascias. A mat of heart-shaped green leaves. 15 × 20cm/6 × 8in

Linum 'Gemmell's Hybrid' Very bright yellow flowers over a neat semi-evergreen dome. ○, E, 15 × 20cm/ 6 × 8in

Pulsatilla vulgaris The flowers of the Pasque flower are followed by beautiful feathery seed heads. ○, 30 × 30cm/1 × 1ft

◆ *There are lovely white, red, pink and pale lavender forms.*

RAISED BEDS

Gentiana sino-ornata An autumn-flowering gentian demanding moist, acid soil in sun. 7.5 × 23cm/3 × 9in

Delosperma nubigenum A rarely grown plant with tender-looking green leaves. Surprisingly hardy. ◯, E, 2.5 × 30cm/1in × 1ft

Euphorbia myrsinites drapes itself over the edge of a raised bed. Attractive at all seasons. ◯, E, 15 × 60cm/6in × 2ft

Ramonda myconi is an ideal plant for the shady side of a peat-block wall. ●, E, 7.5 × 15cm/3 × 6in

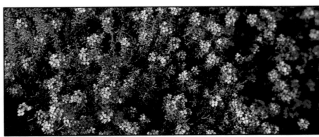

Aethionema 'Warley Rose' A neat little semi-evergreen shrub covered in pink flowers in early summer. ◯, 15 × 23cm/6 × 9in

◆ *Take cuttings to ensure replacement for this short-lived plant.*

On chalk, make raised beds for lime-hating plants with peat-block walls and ericaceous compost.

Gardening can be enjoyed from a wheel-chair using narrow raised beds with a foot recess.

Crepis incana Pink dandelion flowers are seen at their best in a raised bed. ◯, 20 × 45cm/8in × 1½ft

◆ *It does not seed about like a dandelion.*

Sempervivum (Houseleek) Evergreen fleshy rosettes look at home in the crevices of a sunny stone wall.

A BORDER ON TOP OF A TERRACED WALL in a sloping garden, or a raised island bed in an otherwise flat garden adds another dimension in design. Small alpine plants are better appreciated nearer the eye and can be provided with the soil and conditions appropriate to their special needs.

RAISED BEDS

A raised bed made with railway sleepers. *Erysimum* 'Bowles Mauve', helianthemums, saxifrages, pinks and the strikingly variegated *Sisyrinchium striatum* 'Aunt May' jostle happily together.

◆ *All sorts of materials can be used to build retaining walls. Brick and stone are traditional.*

3. Shady Beds

A placid oasis of green shade. Hostas, ferns and white flowers make a place to linger long on a hot afternoon.

A Shady Wall

Jasminum nudiflorum (Winter jasmine), will grow and flower very well against a shady wall.

Sarcococca (Sweet box) is a neat evergreen shade-loving shrub with highly scented winter flowers.

A BORDER AGAINST THE SHADY WALL of a house may need watering occasionally in a dry summer. It is an ideal sheltered spot for plants that like deep shade. The filigree green leaves of ferns and white flowers look particularly good in this situation.

Arum italicum italicum A spectacular foliage plant for winter. Summer-dormant. ●, 25 × 20cm/ 10 × 8in

◆ *These elegant leaves last well in water when picked.*

The climbing **Hydrangea anomala** ssp. **petiolaris** flowers in early summer and reveals its interesting bark and habit in winter. The huge, shiny, tropical-looking leaves of **Fatsia japonica** belie the hardiness of this evergreen shrub. Hostas are at their happiest in shade and ferns revel in such conditions. A dainty form of the lady fern contrasts with the more robust evergreen soft shield fern. A little variegated strawberry weaves about the border.

PLANTING *under* TREES

FEW PLANTS WILL THRIVE in the dense, dry shade of large mature trees but ivy in its many forms grows well to form a dense attractive ground-cover. Smaller deciduous garden trees allow more adventurous planting in their lighter shade. Violets, hellebores and many of the small spring bulbs do well, flowering as they do before the trees come into leaf.

Polygonatum × hybridum Solomon's seal has elegant curving stems from which hang little white bell-shaped flowers. 1m × 45cm/3 × 1½ft

Watch out for cut-worm caterpillars on the foliage of Solomon's seal after flowering.

Plants will require watering regularly until well established after which they will be self-sufficient.

Cyclamen hederifolium Winter-hardy, marbled, ivy-shaped leaves follow the tiny flowers of autumn. 10 × 20cm/4 × 8in

Lamium maculatum album This white-flowered, variegated dead-nettle quickly spreads. 15 × 60cm/6in × 2ft

Euphorbia amygdaloides var. **robbiae** A tough plant to flower well in the deepest and driest shade. E, 60 × 60cm/2 × 2ft

Smilacina racemosa Fluffy white flower spikes at the end of graceful arching stems. Splendid foliage. 75 × 75cm/2½ × 2½ft

◆ *Smilacina grows best in acid soil but will tolerate lime.*

Anemone nemerosa 'Robinsoniana' A cool lavender-blue wood-anemone flowering in late spring. Naturalizes well. 15 × 30cm/6in × 1ft

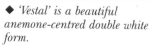

◆ *'Vestal' is a beautiful anemone-centred double white form.*

Iris foetidissima Large seed pods on the Gladwin iris open to reveal bright orange seeds in winter. E, 45 × 60cm/1½ × 2ft

Convallaria majalis Lily-of-the-valley grown for its delicious scent in spring. 20 × 20cm/8 × 8in

◆ *Lovely to pick for the house.*

Lilium martagon var. **album** The easily grown white form of Turk's cap lily. 1.2m × 30cm/4 × 1ft

Symphytum 'Hidcote Blue' A vigorous colonizing comfrey suited to use as ground-cover. 45 × 60cm/ 1½ × 2ft

Dicentra 'Spring Morning' flowers from spring well into summer. Dainty fern-like foliage. 45 × 45cm/ 1½ × 1½ft

Ferns with their lacy foliage make sympathetic companions for all these shade lovers.

Lily-of-the-valley is difficult to eradicate once established, so plant in the right place!

MOIST BEDS *in* SEMI-SHADE

MOIST SHADE IS A RARE COMMODITY but at the bottom of a slope on heavy soil or alongside a natural stream or pond you may have it. It can be created artificially with a porous hose laid on or below the surface connected to a water supply. There are many beautiful plants that revel in these conditions, as do weeds!

Erythronium 'Pagoda' A summer-dormant, spring-flowering tuberous plant. Pale yellow, reflexed, lily-like flowers over glossy foliage. 30 × 20cm/1ft × 8in

If you want to move erythroniums, wait until late summer when they are dormant.

Good plant associations often occur naturally when you plant subjects with similar cultural requirements together.

Corydalis flexuosa may become dormant if dry, but will shoot again as conditions improve.

Primula pulverulenta The flowers are arranged in tiers around the stem, hence the colloquial name of candelabra primula. Shades of dark pink, pink and white harmonize beautifully. 60 × 45cm/2 × 1ft

Primula vialii A unique primula with tightly packed spikes of purple and red. 30 × 20cm/1ft × 8in

Dodecatheon meadia f. **album** A hardy little shooting star with pendant flowers having reflexed petals. 20 × 15cm/8 × 6in

Corydalis flexuosa 'Père David' Dainty fern-like foliage above which dance clear blue spurred flowers. 30 × 30cm/1 × 1ft

Brunnera macrophylla pulmonarioides Forget-me-not flowers over bold green foliage. 45 × 60cm/1½ × 2ft

Mertensia virginica Graceful trumpet-flowers in spring dangle above blue-green foliage that dies down in summer. 60 × 45cm/ 2 × 1½ft

Trollius europaeus Incurved globe flowers of cool lemon yellow over good foliage for early summer. 60 × 45cm/ 2 × 1½ft

Carex elata 'Aurea' Bowles' golden sedge needs some sun for brightest coloured foliage. 60 × 60cm/2 × 2ft

The feathery flowers and foliage of astilbe are the perfect foil for the bold-leaved hosta.

◆ *Plants requiring similar conditions frequently look good together.*

MOIST BEDS *in* SEMI-SHADE

Hyacinthoides non-scripta A patch of bluebells will scent the air in early summer. 30 × 10cm/1ft × 4in

Astrantia major has flowers like little green, white and pink Victorian posies. 60 × 45cm/2 × 1½ft

4. PLANTER'S PALETTE

Plant a perfect picture by blending subtle tones of flower and foliage and providing drama with brighter and contrasting hues.

A border of pink and lilac flowers looks charming in the soft light of late summer and autumn. This group of late-flowering perennials will be in bloom for many weeks. *Anemone* **'September Charm'** with its simple, pink flowers and the elegant bright lavender-blue spikes of *Perovskia atriplicifolia* are complemented by the filigree silver leaves of *Artemisia* **'Powis Castle'**. Cyclamen and low-growing asters are in the foreground.

AFTER THE SHARP GREENS AND YELLOWS OF SPRING the pale pinks, mauves and blues of early summer create a peaceful, harmonious interlude. The planting can be enlivened with accents of a darker hue such as purple or magenta. The pastels themselves will appear deeper if silver foliage and a few white flowers are included.

Hardy chrysanthemums are ideal plants for the autumn border. Try *Dendranthema* 'Clara Curtis', a single pink.

Kolkwitzia amabilis Pink, yellow-centred flowers smother the beauty bush in early summer. ○, 3 × 3m/ 10 × 10ft

Lavatera '**Barnsley**' A fast-growing, short-lived shrub. It flowers continuously throughout the summer. ○, 2 × 1.2m/6 × 4ft

Aster × frikartii A mildew-free Michaelmas daisy flowering from midsummer until autumn. ○, 75 × 60cm/2½ × 2ft

Geranium pratense '**Mrs Kendall Clark**' An attractive, pale form of the meadow cranesbill. 75 × 45cm/2½ × 1½ft

Phlox carolina '**Bill Baker**' A clump-forming, early summer flowering, dwarf phlox. 30 × 30cm/1 × 1ft

◆ *This plant will grow in sun or part shade.*

197

BRIGHT YELLOWS

Lilium 'King Pete' An easily grown hybrid lily. All lilies require good drainage. 60 × 20cm/2ft × 8in

Remove the insignificant flowers of *Valeriana phu* 'Aurea' because any seedlings will have green foliage.

The bright yellow daisies of helenium, heliopsis and inula are good for late summer borders.

Yellow variegated forms of holly or *Euonymus fortunei* have year-round bright foliage.

Euphorbia polychroma bursts into flower in late spring with a long-lasting display of yellow and green bracts. 45 × 60cm/1½ × 2ft

◆ *Forget-me-nots (myosotis) are a lovely combination with this euphorbia.*

Genista hispanica forms a perfectly domed, very prickly green bush. This Spanish gorse covers itself profusely with flowers in early summer. ○, 75cm × 1.2m/2½ × 4ft

Narcissus 'Tête-à-Tête' One of the best little cyclamineus hybrids for early spring. Buttercup-yellow trumpets, often two to a stem. Increases rapidly to make a good clump. 20 × 15cm/ 8 × 6in

◆ *'Tête-à-Tête' is ideal for a raised bed or rock garden. Try it with* Crocus chrysanthus *'Blue Pearl'.*

YELLOW IS CHEERFUL AND ATTRACTS ATTENTION. It is enhanced by good green foliage and a few white flowers. The bright shades of yellow harmonise with the hot oranges and orange-reds of late summer to make a very bright border. Year-long interest can be achieved by planting shrubs with yellow or variegated leaves.

Iris pallida **'Variegata'** retains the beauty of its leaves throughout the summer. ○, 45 × 30cm/ 1½ × 1ft

Valeriana phu **'Aurea'** Eye-catching bright yellow leaves for early spring. ○, 20 × 30cm/8in × 1ft

Euonymus **'Emerald 'n' Gold'** and *Cedrus deodara* **'Golden Horizon'** provide year-long colour and form. A cut-leaved, golden elder adds summer interest.

◆ *Annual poached-egg plant* (Limnanthes douglasii) *and perennial* Corydalis lutea *complete the picture.*

PALE YELLOWS

LUMINOUS PALE YELLOWS are useful for softening a bright scheme and show up well at dusk. A border of pale yellow complemented by shades of pale lilac is very restful. It can be made more exciting by strengthening the lilac shades to purple or magenta.

Phygelius aequalis **'Yellow Trumpet'** A long-flowering summer shrub best planted against a sunny wall. ○, 1.2 × 1.2m/4 × 4ft

Tulipa **'Fringed Elegance'** A fine tulip with a crystal-like fringe. ○, 40 × 20cm/ 1½ft × 8in

Anthemis tinctoria **'Alba'** A pale, creamy form of this floriferous perennial. Cut down after flowering. ○, 75 × 75cm/2½ × 2½ft

Primula vulgaris A double form of the common primrose and a favourite flower for spring. 15 × 20cm/6 × 8in

A successful, cool looking border using green and silver foliage and contrasting textures in flower and leaf. Cream and pale yellow flowers are enhanced by a touch of contrasting purple.

A pleasing association of pale yellow and lilac flowers: *Alcea rugosa* (a perennial hollyhock), *Penstemon* **'Alice Hindley'** and *Clematis* **'Perle d'Azur'** of slightly darker hue, are good companions.

◆ *These shades can also be combined in a spring border using narcissus, crocus and tulips.*

Kniphofia 'Little Maid' A dainty little red hot poker that is not red! Ideal for a small garden. Creamy yellow spikes rise above grassy foliage. 60 × 45cm/ 2 × 1½ft

◆ *Lilac-blue Aster thomsonii 'Nanus' is a good companion for this late-flowering kniphofia.*

Rosa **'The Pilgrim'** A modern English rose with flat petal-packed blooms like the old gallicas. 1 × 1m/3 × 3ft

The silvery artemisias associate well with pale yellow flowers. All need sun and good drainage.

It is wise to give kniphofias a little winter protection with a mulch of straw.

'Maggie Mott' is an easily grown viola of clear violet to associate with these yellows.

HOT REDS

BRIGHT RED IS EYE-CATCHING and appears to bring the border nearer to the viewer. In a small garden this can make the garden itself feel smaller. Planted with bright green foliage the red will seem even brighter. A more subtle effect is achieved by using harmonizing foliage in tones of brown, black and purple.

Dahlia **'Bishop of Llandaff'** The bright flowers are in perfect harmony with the dark bronze foliage. 75 × 45cm/2½ × 1½ft

Helianthemum **'Supreme'** is one of several good rock roses which provide brilliant pools of colour in summer. For well-drained soil. ○, E, 15 × 45cm/6in × 1½ft

Papaver orientale The oriental poppy of early summer. Avoid seedlings by removing seed heads. 1m × 60cm/3 × 2ft

Rosa moyesii Grow this large species rose for its avalanche of red flask-shaped hips. 4 × 3m/ 13 × 10ft

Tulipa **'Apeldoorn'** A vigorous, very hardy tulip of eye-dazzling red. Nice with cream wallflowers. 60 × 20cm/2ft × 8in

Crocosmia **'Lucifer'** A magnificent tall crocosmia whose sword-like leaves retain their good looks throughout the summer. 1.2m × 30cm/4 × 1ft

◆ *Divide this vigorous plant in spring if it becomes congested.*

Cordyline australis
'Purpurea' A temporary tender addition to a border for the summer. ○, E, 1m × 60cm/3 × 2ft

Cotinus coggygria **'Royal Purple'** This smoke bush is a lovely background shrub for any border. 4 × 4m/ 13 × 13ft

Phormium tenax **'Purpureum' (New Zealand flax)** In a sheltered spot this plant will look smart. ○, E, 1.5 × 1.2m/5 × 4ft

Penstemon **'Red Knight'** Encourage repeat flowering by cutting out stems that have finished flowering. ○, E, 75 × 45cm/2½ × 1½ft

Euphorbia dulcis **'Chameleon'** Brownish purple leaves of summer turn orange-red in autumn. 40 × 40cm/16 × 16in

HOT REDS

·Dahlias need lifting in autumn and storing almost dry in frost-free conditions.

Cordylines look well placed in the border still in their pots, which give added height.

A background of tall purple-leaved shrubs against which are displayed the scintillating reds of *Lobelia cardinalis*, dahlias and annual tobacco plants.

◆ *The red flowers and foliage are enhanced by the surrounding greens.*

203

COOL WHITES

WHITE FLOWERS AND GREEN FOLIAGE look sophisticated and are particularly good in the formal planting of geometric beds. White shows up well in a shady corner and in the evening. A large border planted entirely in white needs a dash of one other colour to enliven it: soft apricot or pale blue works well.

Campanula latiloba alba A bell-flower seen at its best in partial shade.
1.2m × 30cm/4 × 1ft

◆ *Handsome evergreen basal leaves are a winter bonus.*

Phlox divaricata **'May Breeze'** has deliciously scented white flowers in early summer. 30 × 20cm/ 1ft × 8in

◆ *This is a lovely cool-looking plant for shade.*

Lilium regale The regal lily is easily grown, given good drainage and sun.
1.2m × 30cm/4 × 1ft

◆ *This midsummer lily is powerfully scented.*

A beautiful single white **peony, 'White Wings'**, is the star of this early summer border. It is seen against a background of *Crambe cordifolia* with its haze of tiny gypsophila-like flowers. The use of pale apricot **foxgloves** with white avoids the blandness of an entirely white border. White **aquilegias** and *Viola cornuta alba* mingle to complete a tranquil composition.

5. FILLING THE GAPS IN BORDERS

The inevitable gaps that occur in a border provide an excellent opportunity to introduce something temporary.

ANNUALS *and* BIENNIALS

THESE PLANTS ARE EASILY GROWN FROM SEED and are useful for filling large gaps in new borders. Annuals flower in their first year and biennials in their second. Many will self-seed *in situ* and are invaluable for growing in gaps that occur where spring bulbs have died down. Experiment with new ones each year.

Do not pull out lunaria, nigella or opium poppies after flowering, they make attractive seed-heads.

Sweet William and love-in-a-mist are good cut flowers as are annual gypsophila and cornflowers.

Gilia capitata An unusual, dainty annual toning well with delphiniums which flower at the same time. ○, 45 × 20cm/1½ft × 8in

These delicate, slender, annual **Shirley poppies** bloom in midsummer. They have developed from the red field poppy, *Papaver rhoeas*. Allow to self-seed for next year.

◆ Papaver somniferum, *the opium poppy, a larger sturdier poppy, has superb seed-heads*.

Nicotiana langsdorffii A green-flowered tobacco plant with a long, narrow, bell-shaped flower. 1m × 30cm/3 × 1ft

Nigella damascena **('Love-in-a-mist')** Useful for a blue and white planting scheme. Self-seeds discreetly. 45 × 20cm/1½ft × 8in

Cosmos A long-flowering, tall annual. Raise in pots to fill unexpected gaps in the borders. 1m × 60cm/3 × 2ft

Dianthus barbatus An auricula-eyed Sweet William gives an old-fashioned look to early summer borders. ◯, 45 × 30cm/1½ × 1ft

Salvia sclarea var. ***turkestanica*** A dominant biennial with big hairy leaves and lavender-purple bracts. 75 × 30cm/2½ × 1ft

Myosotis alpestris There are also pink and white forms of the forget-me-not. 30 × 30cm/1 × 1ft

***Lunaria annua* 'Alba Variegata'** This white-flowered, variegated biennial honesty is unusual. 75 × 30cm/2½ × 1ft

Many annuals make sturdier plants if sown in autumn, as they would be in the wild.

Look out for self-sown annuals when you are weeding in spring and avoid the hoe.

Limnanthes douglasii The poached-egg plant is a good front row annual for a sunny spot. 15 × 15cm/ 6 × 6in

Cheiranthus cheiri Grow wallflowers as biennials. Good mixers with all spring bulbs. 45 × 30cm/1½ × 1ft

Calendula officinalis Marigolds are usually orange but paler shades of apricot and cream are available. ◯, 45 × 30cm/ 1½ × 1ft

HALF-HARDY PERENNIALS

Pelargonium 'Velvet Duet'
One of the little pelargoniums of the Angel group, with flowers like violas. They make charming gap-fillers. ○, 20 × 20cm/ 8 × 8in

Argyranthemum 'Vancouver' Paris daisies or marguerites have pink, white or yellow, single or double daisies in abundance. ○, 1 × 1m/ 3 × 3ft

Osteospermum 'Buttermilk'
Cool pale yellow petals fading towards the dark centre are unusual. ○, 60 × 30cm/2 × 1ft

◆ *Remove flowers as they die to encourage more.*

Arctotis × hybrida 'Apricot'
Red, white and yellow African daisies are good for 'hot' summer beds. ○, 45 × 30cm/1½ × 1ft

Use pelargoniums (commonly known as geraniums) in shades that are sympathetic to their bed-fellows.

Sphaeralcea munroana makes a mat of foliage covered in flowers all summer. *S. fendleri* is a paler pink. ○, 30cm × 1m/1 × 3ft

THESE PLANTS MAKE A VALUABLE CONTRIBUTION to the summer border, flowering with abundance all season long. They are not winter-hardy so need to be propagated from cuttings every year in late summer and over-wintered in a frost-free greenhouse. Alternatively the plants may be dug up, re-potted and given similar protection.

Cosmos atrosanguineus A curiosity: dark reddish-brown flowers smelling of chocolate. ○, 60 × 45cm/ 2 × 1½ft

Heliotropium peruvianum Plant this beside a seat on the terrace where its scent can be appreciated. 60 × 60cm/2 × 2ft

Solanum rantonnetii makes a sizeable free-flowering shrub in one year from cuttings. ○, 1.5 × 1.2m/ 5 × 4ft

◆ *This looks best in a border against a wall.*

Felicia amelloides A wonderful clear blue, yellow-centred daisy. ○, 45 × 45cm/1½ × 1½ft

BULBS *and* TUBERS

BULBS ADD AN ELEMENT OF SURPRISE IN A BORDER: they appear when we have forgotten that we have planted them! Hardy bulbs such as daffodils are left in the soil and multiply to make big clumps. Tender subjects such as dahlias and gladioli will need to be lifted in autumn and given winter protection.

Tulipa **'Purissima'** Perfect with yellow polyanthus and good dark green foliage. ○, 40 × 20cm/16 × 8in

Narcissus **'Rip van Winkle'** A tough little double daffodil, perfect for a raised bed. It multiplies rapidly. 15 × 15cm/6 × 6in

Gladiolus byzantinus An early gladiolus that can be left in the ground. The later, more flamboyant grandiflorus and primulinus gladioli are not hardy. ○, 60 × 15cm/2ft × 6in

Order your bulbs early in the season to ensure that you get those you want.

Allium christophii Huge spectacular flower heads. Try to place a low plant in front to disguise the allium foliage which always becomes untidy. ○, 45 × 20cm/1½ft × 8in

◆ *The seed-heads dry perfectly and are much sought after by flower arrangers.*

212

Fritillaria imperialis A
stately spring bulb for
good well-drained soil in
sun or partial shade.
Crown imperials have a
ring of orange, red or
yellow flowers on tall leafy
stems, crowned with a tuft
of leaves. The bulbs
should be planted on their
sides with some coarse
sand. 1.5m × 30cm/5 × 1ft

Fritillaria persica A
sophisticated fritillary
with a fascinating grape-
like bloom on its leaves
and its purple-black
flowers. A challenge to
grow in rich, well-
drained soil in sun. ◯,
75 × 30cm/2½ × 1ft

CLIMBERS

Eccremocarpus scaber A long succession of red, yellow or orange flowers for full sun. Easy to grow from seed which is produced in abundance. 3m/10ft

The sweet pea, *Lathyrus odoratus*, is an excellent annual climber to grow on a bamboo wig-wam.

Canary creeper (*Tropaeolum peregrinum*) is a yellow flowered, fast-growing annual climber with attractive leaves.

Clematis texensis hybrids, with their tulip-shaped flowers, are ideal to grow through winter heathers.

Clematis alpina **'Pamela Jackman'** is seen here climbing through the new variegated leaves of *Sambucus nigra* 'Marginata'. No regular pruning is required but it may be cut back immediately after flowering. 2m/6ft

◆ Clematis macropetala *is similar but has semi-double flowers. Pink and white forms of both available.*

Humulus lupulus 'Aureus' A wonderful, yellow-leaved form of hop making vigorous sprawling annual growth. In a small garden confine it to a pole. 4m/13ft

CLIMBING PLANTS are generally grown on a wall or fence at the back of the border or up a pole or obelisk to add height. Less formally they can be used to scramble into established shrubs or allowed to sprawl forwards to cover the dying foliage of earlier flowers.

Tropaeolum speciosum (**Flame creeper**) Often seen adorning yew hedges and favouring cool, moist, acid soils. 3m/10ft

Clematis × durandii has a very long flowering season. Lovely scrambling through *Brachyglottis* 'Sunshine'. 1.5 × 1.5m/5 × 5ft

Lathyrus rotundifolius The Persian everlasting pea has early summer flowers of an unusual shade of soft brick red. 2m/6ft

◆ *Unfortunately this decorative pea has no perfume.*

This very formal border alongside a shady path uses repetition of identically planted urns to achieve unity. *Hedera helix* **'Parsley Crested'** is the ivy used. Spilling across the path are *Hosta* **'Thomas Hogg'** and *Alchemilla mollis*. The ivy will look good at all seasons but will be the dominant feature in winter when the herbaceous plants are dormant.

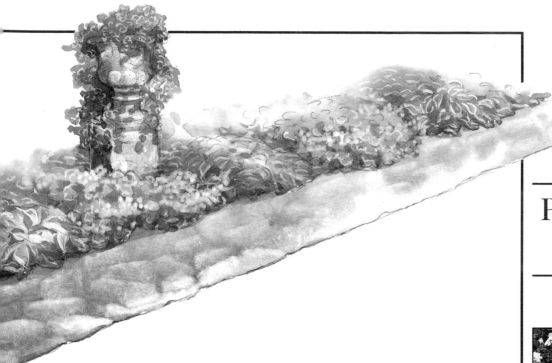

UNEXPECTED GAPS IN BORDERS can be filled with plants kept in reserve in pots: lilies and hostas are excellent for this purpose. The pots give added height and importance to the plants. In a formal setting large terracotta pots will reinforce the formality and can be replanted seasonally.

A shallow pot, planted with silver saxifrages, has been raised on a plinth to give it more importance.

The lilies in this border are growing in a large pot. When they have finished flowering they can be replaced by a later flowering lily.

◆ *It is important to remember to water plants in pots used in borders.*